How I Came to Christ

How I Came to Christ

SUNIL SHARAN

RESOURCE *Publications* · Eugene, Oregon

HOW I CAME TO CHRIST

Resource Publications
An Imprint of Wipf and Stock Publishers
199 W. 8th Ave., Suite 3
Eugene, OR 97401

www.wipfandstock.com

PAPERBACK ISBN: 978-1-6667-0009-1
HARDCOVER ISBN: 978-1-6667-0010-7
EBOOK ISBN: 978-1-6667-0011-4

04/28/21

Contents

Introduction

I am 52. I was born and raised Hindu in India, although like tens of millions of my peers I attended a Jesuit missionary convent school almost my entire childhood. Convent schools are held in high regard in India even today. They provide a solid grounding in English, which is the language on which basis the country runs. If your English is poor in India, you might as well remain a shop-keeper all your life.

There is another facet for which Indians of all faiths send their kids to the convents. There is a subject called Moral Science there. In the Moral Science period, students are taught about aspects of Christianity. After so many years, perhaps the only takeaway that I can remember from those periods was developing a conscience. Perhaps that was more than enough.

Hardly any of the students attending the convents get converted to Christianity, although some get influenced heavily. My only sister is two years older than me. As my father was tucking her into bed one night, she said that she believed in Christianity. My father was taken aback. He told her that you should believe in your own religion i.e. Hinduism, although you should respect all religions. This was in conformity with the secular ethos of India that persists unto this day. My sister, reassured, went to sleep.

The Indian Constitution allows for proselytization. This has presented a dilemma for the country. The majority religion, Hinduism, does not evangelize as a rule. Minority religions like Christianity, Islam, and Buddhism do. Christianity's way of conversion since the Europeans brought the religion in a big way to the country has mostly always been subtle—through education, medical care and other social services. The natives of India were strongly wed to their religion, Hinduism. I remember reading about a pastor of the eighteenth century saying that it would take a stick to beat Hinduism out of the natives' ear drums.

Mercifully, for the main part, Christians in India did not employ this route. Yes, the English were downright racist and plundered the country dry, but their religion inspired people like Mahatma Gandhi and Swami Vivekananda, one of Hinduism's holiest saints who travelled to America, twice, at the turn of the nineteenth century.

As such one does not find the discord in India between Christianity and Hinduism that one sees between Islam and Hinduism there today. Muslims have contributed to India in many ways—architecture, language, cuisine—but in the matter of proselytization they seem to have taken heavy-handed measures thereby alienating Hindu sensibilities.

Still, India is an eighty-percent majority Hindu country and a fervent Hindu country. Any convert to Islam, and even Christianity, is seen with suspicion. Conversion can break bonds with your family. You can be rendered an outcaste. You might even face discrimination. But then religion and spirituality are matters of the soul. The choice before man and mankind is vast and varied. It is whatever that clicks for you. Some people ask God for temporal gifts. In my case, I have seldom asked God for anything. But being a devout Hindu for twenty years was only bringing misery, disease, poverty, hunger, and social ostracization in my life. There had to be a better path for me to follow. In my forties I started to engage with the Light—Christ—that I had done so in my formative years. I just asked for His Will to be done in my life. I found more solace and less confusion and more clarity with Him. This book relates my journey, an ongoing one, towards Jesus Christ, My One and Only LORD and Savior now.

CHAPTER 1

Holli

Sometimes one looks back in life and wonders what might have been. In 2001, I was 32 and flying to Jackson, Mississippi, with Nils, my favorite colleague. Nils was about 55 and a man of the Christian faith, but he never forced it down your throat. He was a sales guy and had a sales guy's sense of humor and interest in women. I just loved traveling with him.

Two rows in front of us sat a pretty single woman. I dumped Nils and plonked myself right next to her. Nils chuckled. I had the girl captive to myself for a couple hours. I didn't want the flight to end. She went by Holli and lived in Jackson. I could see that she was blushing pink. Either she was embarrassed by all the attention that I was lavishing on her or she had developed the hots for me. We would find out. I made sure to take her number and email address.

Once the flight landed, Nils guffawed. He said you see a pretty bird and leave me stranded. I responded, well, I am in the marriage market and I am going to get nothing from you in that regard.

The same year, 2001, my father was visiting me from India. I lived in California then, as I do now. I got busy tending to my dad and forgot all about Holli. I was still in touch with my ex, Sonya. We had remained friends and confidantes after we had parted ways. Sonya used to constantly counsel me to read the classics.

One day, my boss told me to fly to Allentown, Pennsylvania for a conference. Allentown has of course been made famous by the Billy Joel song. I wasn't really looking forward to the trip. The conference was going to be held at a Days Inn, where I would have to stay overnight. I was used to staying at better hotels than Days Inn. Days Inn was infra dig for me.

But this was to be one of those in-and-out conferences. California to anywhere on the East Coast is a six-hour long flight. Six hours to get there, get some food and sleep, make your presentation the following day, and hop back on your flight to California. All pretty much a day's work. Not really the less intense kind of trip that I liked to take. But then California is far away from everywhere. Far away from the East Coast, which is six hours away. Far away from Europe, which is 10 hours away. Far away from India, which is 20 hours away. Go whichever direction you want, over the Atlantic or over the Pacific, it's exactly the same distance to India.

I was supposed to speak at 9:30 am. Prime time. Right after breakfast. Except that I was still groggy because of jet lag. I could only go to sleep around 3 am local time because of the time difference between California and Allentown. And then I had to get up at 6. So I had barely had any sleep. The people visiting the conference from the East Coast and the Midwest were much chipper. I had to play along. I was in sales and marketing after all. Lots of backslapping and sucking up was going on. Around 9 though, things turned dark. Someone talked about planes hitting buildings. My presentation was cancelled. 9/11 had struck.

I saw the twin towers come crashing down. I had an electronic device with me that resembled a bomb. I called my boss in California. He said that the fallout of this 9/11 incident was not ending anytime soon, and allowed me to FedEx the device home. My industry mates from Chicago pooled a car and got out of Allentown. When I asked to take a ride with them to Chicago, they refused. And then how was I going to get from Chicago to California? No flights were operating. I decided to stay on in the Days Inn.

I had brought along a copy of *War and Peace* with me. It was a massive tome, even the paperback version that I had. I went to the front desk and told them that I would be staying with them until flights started operating. But every day when I tried to check into my room after breakfast, my keycard wouldn't operate. I would have to return to the front desk for help. One clerk asked me how long I was going to stay at the hotel. I responded until I could get a flight out. But this drama kept happening every day. It seemed obvious that they didn't want me there.

The hotel was owned by an Indian, who stayed in deep background. So I bore up with the daily indignity. It always boggles, as well as boils, my mind that Americans in general are so welcoming to people of all creeds and colors and let non-Christian people freely practice their faith, but that there are still quite a few bad eggs out floating somewhere in America. It only takes one rotten apple to spoil the entire basket.

Pennsylvania is a beautiful state. Summer was seeping out, fall was setting in. It was a beautiful time of year. I took to going to the gym across the road. It was made fully of wood. I marveled at the ingenuity of the people who had built it with so much care and expense. And then I remembered. I needed to email Holli.

My hotel didn't have an Internet connection, so I walked to a nearby library and emailed her. Everyone everywhere was kind and welcoming. I didn't feel anywhere that I was being targeted. Holli wrote back soon enough. Soon we became like pen pals, sending emails back and forth. I was young and agile then and could walk for miles. I took to walking in the Pennsylvania woods. I would walk for miles. One day there was a vintage car rally. Everyone waved at me as they passed. I didn't detect any hostility. It was as if 9/11 had never even happened. Americans are a resilient people. They don't mope around; they get on with their lives.

Flights resumed after eight days. I was glad to get out. Yes, I had struck a rapport with Holli, but my dad was stuck in Las Vegas, and I needed to get back home to receive him. My older brother was already raising Cain over my dad. The clerk who had given me the hardest time was now apologetic for her behavior.

She drove me to Philadelphia airport. That was kind. I got on my flight. Along came a middle-aged American man who sat next to me.

I, somewhat foolishly, asked him what he thought about what was going on. He made one of the most sensible statements that I have ever heard. He said that this thing—this inter-religious warfare—has been going on for a thousand years and will go on for a thousand more. I reached home without much further ado.

Things with Holli were heating up. She told me that she was Christian. Sonya asked me to ask her her Christian denomination. Sonya didn't want it to be Baptist because she felt that they were too orthodox. It wasn't. Holli was Methodist. I didn't know one from the other. Holli's dad, Bob, called me at my office. I shut the door. He said that the problem was how your kids with Holli would be raised. Was I willing to convert to Christianity? I said I would do so, but slowly. He was unconvinced.

Holli clearly liked me. But then tragedy struck. My dad went home to India in November and passed away shortly thereafter. It was a shock. I rushed home for the funeral rites. His last wish was that I get married. I was presented with the profiles of three girls in India. I chose the prettiest. I didn't realize then that she was also the most uneducated and the most provincial.

I brought my wife with me to the States. My life was soon to turn upside down. My wife had forged her educational certificates. She could barely speak a word of English. She couldn't cook. She was terrified of intimacy. I complained to my mom. She said that I had to grin and bear it. I told Holli that I had gotten married.

I was applying to MBA programs and wanted someone to edit my application essays. Holli's English was very good. I asked her to review my essays. She did a mighty fine job of it, although she didn't support me going back to school. She was of the feeling that I was doing well in life already and that I been through multiple life-changing experiences and that I should not introduce more change into my life.

I asked her how I should pay her for the essays. Would she like shoes? She said which girl doesn't like shoes. But I realized I was being cheap. I needed to reimburse her as if she was a professional. The going rate for a professional was $60 an hour. I paid her what was due her and felt happy doing so.

Holli was clearly still in love with me. She said that her heart had been taken by a Christian preacher of Indian origin. He was Ravi Zacharias. She sent me a book of his, *Jesus Among Other Gods*. It talked about Hindu gods as being false gods. I was offended. Hinduism was too ingrained in my system then. Now of course I know better. I got busy trying to manage my marriage and didn't hear anymore from Holli.

My marriage had started in January 2002. I filed for divorce two and half years later. I then wrote Holli an email. Was she still waiting for me? Her father, Bob, replied. He said that she had been betrothed to someone else. I wish I had seen the Light earlier. I would probably have still been married to her with two or three kids by now. Kids of mixed American-Indian parentage look gorgeous. In Hindu culture, divorce is frowned upon. Even though I had only a little role to play in arranging my bad marriage, my family has actively connived in me not getting remarried. It was as if I had done a crime by getting divorced. Hindu culture does not allow one to redeem oneself. At 52, I am single, and without any kids.

I am still looking for a woman of child-bearing age. Good luck with that! Holli would happily have moved to California to live with me. She said one thing that grated on me then, but doesn't do so now. She said that the US was getting corrupted, so to speak, by letting so many people of different faiths in. I agree with her now. I feel that Christianity is the bedrock of the US. If people of different creeds come here, and practice their own diverse faiths, the US will not remain what it is. This is not some kind of xenophobic or even Islamophobic statement. It is purely a statement of fact. The US was built on Christian endeavor. Let's try to keep it that way.

Almost two decades later, I wonder where Holli is, this pretty Christian girl I was ready to marry even without kissing her. Is she happy with her man? Does she have kids? How does she look now? I have never tried to contact her and neither has she tried to contact me. In fact, I have even misplaced her email address even though it was not hard to remember. It might be good to get together and reminisce about old times, about what might have been. But if the LORD, Jesus Christ, had meant to bring us together, He would have made it happen. Holli has faded from my memory, but not her kindness, her sensibility and above all her faith. I still keep the Ravi Zacharias book with me as a memento of our relationship. It's one of my most prized possessions. I have read it from cover to cover.

CHAPTER 2

My Early Life

My father was an Indian army officer. As is typical with any army, my father (and his family) were rotated from army base to army base. In India, we call an army base a cantonment. The British built these cantonments adjacent to but isolated from the teeming civilian towns and cities. Just in case the natives decided to rebel, the British could call on the military forces quickly to quell the uprising. Now of course after the British left and the Indians took over, the towns and cities are not expected to rebel, but the cantonment structure continues.

I was the youngest of three kids. At age three, I pleaded with my mother to send me to school. I saw my older brother and sister going to school and wanted to be like them. My mother found a convent kindergarten for me. Let me explain what a convent school in India is. It is typically a Catholic school run by Jesuit missionaries. In British times, many of these came from Ireland. Over time, control of the schools passed on to Anglo-Indians.

When the British came to India in the eighteenth century, they were all male. As they conquered and settled different parts of India, they felt the need for female intimacy. Female intimacy for them was mainly available in the native dancing halls, which also served as brothels. From this miscegenation rose a mixed race, the Anglo-Indian, half-British, half-Indian. British females, also known as *memsahibs* (mem is a derivative of Ma'am, and *sahib* means a lord, so a *memsahib* meant a female lord. The term is still widely used in India to denote rich Indian women) started arriving in India in the nineteenth century when the British had wrested full control of the country. The British women immediately put a stop to the practice of miscegenation between their males and Indian women.

Yet a whole class of mixed-breed Anglo-Indians had developed in India. Their fathers had made sure that they were given Christian names and were raised Christian. Anglo-Indians occupied a status somewhere in between the Brits and the native Indians. They were loyal to the British Crown so the British trusted them more than they trusted the natives. They were given much higher positions in government, even though these were not equivalent to what the British reserved for themselves.

An area in which the Anglo-Indians thrived was education. There were not that many educators and preachers coming to India from Europe to man the Christian schools already in place as well as to expand the school system. The Brits left this task in the hands of the Anglo-Indians. The English of the Anglo-Indians was perfect, they were fervent Christians, and they were loyal to the Crown. As English became the lingua franca of the country, the natives had nowhere else to send their kids to but to convent schools run by Anglo-Indians where the medium of instruction was English.

Christian missionaries in India had learned the hard way that they could not drum out with a heavy hand Hinduism and Islam from the natives. The natives were much too wed to their religious beliefs. Setting up a network of convents throughout the country was a subtle way of spreading Christianity. It was a kinder, gentler way of doing so. The kids, even those of the natives, had to pray to Jesus during the school assembly, sing Christian hymns and go to the school chapel. If a child or two converted, the administrators were happy. But it was a slog. At home, the natives followed their religions fervently. So the child was exposed to Christianity at school, and her parent's religion at home.

In kindergarten, I had an Anglo-Indian language teacher who loved me. She gave me aces on all my tests. My mother was mightily pleased. Soon we had to move to the northern Indian town of Ambala. I was now all of four, in the first grade. I attended the Rachna Montessori school, a network of schools that is part of the Montessori school system. My principal called me sweetheart. I loved her for it. Rachna schooled only until the second grade, so I had to transfer to the Convent of Jesus & Mary in the same town for my third grade. My older sister went to the same school. She used to pick me up after school and we used to board the school bus together to go home. I would wait beside a particular tree for her. One afternoon she forgot to show up. I waited by the tree, petrified. Minutes seemed to become hours. I saw the whole school leave, all the nuns and the teachers and the students.

I was left alone by the tree. I started bawling. I thought, had my sister abandoned me for life? I dare not move from the tree or ask anyone for help. Fortunately, after three hours, the batman (an orderly assigned by the Indian army as domestic help in an army officer's house) showed up on his bicycle. I didn't talk to my sister for days. As I remember it, she was rather unrepentant. Still, my class teacher adored me. When my father got transferred from Ambala, my class teacher gave me a bunch of treats. She told my mother that if I had been her age, she would have married me instantly. My mother still chuckles at that statement.

We moved to a remote northeastern town in India called Tezpur. My parents put my sister and me in a convent once again. I went to an all-boys convent called St. Joseph's convent. The class teacher in the fourth grade didn't take a shine to me. The school enforced that every student learn the local language, Assamese. I had no knowledge of it. My mother begged the nuns that we were army folks and that we moved from place to place, so how could we be expected to know the local dialect. The nuns relented and let me learn a watered-down version of the language.

My class teacher announced that someone had stood first in the class, but wouldn't reveal his identity. It was obviously me. She had taken a real antipathy towards me. This behavior was hard for me to digest. I had always been the beloved of all my teachers before then. What was I doing wrong? I went to the chapel and prayed. For myself and for my father, who was drinking heavily at the time because of a bad turn of fortune in his career.

After I finished my fifth grade, I was glad to be out of St. Joseph's. I spent the sixth grade at a secular school. I really didn't like it. I missed my morning assembly, the singing of Christian hymns, and the prayer to Jesus. I missed the solace and the spiritual nourishment that going to the school chapel provided. Finally my father was transferred to Pune, a town in the west of India that was close to Bombay (now Mumbai).

Even though I didn't realize it then, young as I was, I was slowly coming close to Jesus. I felt more close to Him than to any Hindu god. But I was still a child, and I was finding my way in life in so many things. Spirituality was only one of them. In Pune, my father had a choice of sending me to two different convents: St. Vincent's or Bishop's High. Army officers had sparse salaries and most sent their kids to the less expensive St. Vincent's but my father chose Bishop's High. It was an all-boy's school. I was in an all-boy's school once again. My sister attended the neighboring sister school, St. Mary's, just a stone's throw away. But we were not allowed to mingle with the girls there.

The vice-principal of Bishop's and head of the middle school was a fair-skinned classic Anglo-Indian 70-year old man called Mr. Ringrow. We boys called him KingCrow. Every teacher had a nick name. My class teacher in the seventh grade was rather heavy, so we used to call him Jumbo to his face. KingCrow used to teach us history. In a few weeks, he warned the topper of the class, a boy called Chadha, that Chadha & Co. you have new competition, that is, from me. Chadha was the gang leader of the class. He did his best thereupon to pull me down.

The morning assembly at Bishop's was very strict. They wouldn't let you into the hall if you were late. We had to wear a school uniform including a tie. Everything had to be ship-shape. Monitors from senior classes roamed the assembly hall. They would inspect your nails. If one's nails were out of order, one could expect a sharp rap on the knuckles with a ruler. If one was caught talking in assembly, one could get spanked. Particularly frightening was a Nigerian student in the tenth grade. He was a superb soccer player. But he gave the worst-imaginable two fingered slap on your cheek if he found you going out of line. Those fingers were not only painful but also left indelible marks. V for victory! Of the Nigerian.

The fathers and the teachers allowed the monitors complete leeway in how they treated students under their charge. The school strictly believed in the policy of sparing the rod and spoiling the child. Americans might balk at all the spanking, but that was an integral part of the Jesuit school system in India in the seventies and the eighties. My father too believed in the adage of sparing the rod and spoiling the child even though he never hit me. So it was not as if you could come home and cry about the spanking. It was as if you were sent to a military academy and what happened there remained inside.

But it was not all beatings and spankings. It was a lovely school. Even though India had become independent from the British for over thirty years, the school inculcated a love of things British in us. We read Shakespeare, saw Shakespearean plays, and there was a Duke of Edinburgh award awaiting the best all-round student. It was made out as if the British had only done good to India and no harm.

My father was drinking more and more heavily and I was visiting the school chapel more and more to pray to Jesus to rid my father of the habit. My sister and I walked the same path to school. We never walked together. She was always a few steps in front of me. Along the way was a modest house of her English teacher, a Christian woman who lived alone. My sister was heavily influenced by her. She announced her intention of becoming a nun. Once while my father was tucking her to sleep, she said that she believed in Jesus. My father was taken aback. He responded that one should respect all religions but believe in only one, our Hindu one. I think my sister was very influenced by Christianity.

She came to the States in 1986, when she was just 19, and quickly met and married a Christian man.

My father retired from the army in 1981, and we moved back home to Delhi. I was thrust into a huge secular school, which was almost like a factory school. At Bishop's I was a star. At Delhi Public School (in India private schools are called public schools) I was a nobody. My father had moved to Iraq to work. I was completely lost at school. There was some religious education, but it was in name only. Students showed off money at school. Teachers were more interested in the rich students than in imparting education to all. It was a real culture shock for me. I missed my Christian hymns, the image of Jesus on a cross, and the chapel. But what was I to do? I would dream about Bishop's at night. I badly wanted to return there. I haven't been to Pune in 40 years, but if I go, the first stop for me would be Bishop's.

I want to see the rooms where I spent my seventh and eighth grades. I am sure the school must be completely transformed. It was the school that has had a seminal impact on my life. I would say that most everything I have become in life is because of the Christian education that I imbibed at that school.

Four years, four unhappy years of high school, passed at the Delhi Public School. It was not that I never wanted to go to school. I was keen to go to school every day, but I never really looked forward to it as I had done at Bishop's and at my other convents (barring St. Joseph's). My English teacher in the Delhi Public School was Christian. She noticed that I was withdrawn, shy, and becoming an introvert. She begged me to take part in theatre at school, but I flat out refused. I had shot up a foot in the eleventh grade, was thin and gangly as hell, and extremely conscious of my physique and the color of my skin, which was dark. I wish I had listened to my English teacher. She really cared for me. She had a nervous breakdown, mainly because of bullying from another teacher, a Hindu. It was all so sad. My English teacher imbibed in me a love for the classics. In the twelfth grade, the class had a choice to go with a harder English option and read *Great Expectations* by Charles Dickens or go with a softer option and read a weaker book. The teacher wanted us to choose *Great Expectations*.

I thought that I would score more points with the softer option, and was adamant that we go with it. In the end, I was wrong. I did not do any better with the softer option than I would have done with the harder option. And reading and studying and analyzing *Great Expectations* would have done wonders for my English. Teachers truly know what is better for you.

After I graduated from high school, I gained admission to one of India's premier engineering schools, the Birla Institute of Technology & Science (BITS), Pilani for a five-year dual degree program in physics and electrical engineering. The school is set on a sprawling campus in the west of India. A massive marble Hindu temple with busts of Lincoln and JFK carved on its outside is the center piece of the campus.

When I was growing up, I found that my father had a Bible titled Love on his bookshelf with the Taj Mahal imprinted on the cover. I would open it and try to read it but failed to understand its import. The Bible is still there in my parent's living room. My mother, although Hindu, is an ardently secular woman. There is a big image of Jesus on her prayer altar in the living room. I would sleep in the living room all through my high school and college years and derive succor from the presence of the Bible as well as the image of Jesus there.

In college though, the atmosphere was very Hindu. One of my best friends, Victor, a Christian Anglo-Indian would accompany me to the temple. I missed Jesus, but what could I do? There was where I had to spend five years. Most students used to go to the temple to seek succor before an exam. And almost every student wore slippers (flip-flops) on campus.

These slippers would be massed up outside the temple entrance. These were cheap rubber flip-flops, not costing more than a couple of dollars but many students went to the temple with the express aim of stealing someone else's new slippers and leaving their old ones behind. I found the whole idea repugnant. Are you going to a place of worship to pray to God or with the thought of stealing? I think that many students lacked the Christian concept of conscience and righteousness that I had imbibed in my convent schools. That perhaps also explains the endemic corruption in India, which has a population that is 80% Hindu. Somehow Hinduism is not able to inculcate in its adherents the sense of discerning right from wrong. I feel that the same is the case with Islam and other religions except for Christianity.

BITS though was a very westernized school. It had been founded by the Massachusetts Institute of Technology, so its very foundations were very American. Almost every student wanted to go to the States to study, work and live. Their Indian dream was to partake of the American dream. Once, while I was at BITS, a former prime minister of India passed away. The government declared a national holiday, but the director of the school kept it open. Asked why, he laconically remarked, that BITS was not an Indian school; it was an American school that found itself to be in India.

The American dream on almost every student's mind was fast girls and fast cars, nothing to do with Jesus. Every student thought that as soon as they landed in America, there would be a bevy of white beauties for the handsome Indian guys that they thought they were. Many students from India who come to the US today continue to think that way. Nothing could be further from the truth. All such notions would be disabused upon landing in America, as I was to discover soon. The bevy of white beauties in America would not even give Indians a second glance, let alone have anything else to do with them.

CHAPTER 3

First Exposure
to Protestantism

My father was approaching sixty as I was finishing my gradu-
ation from BITS. He had put his older son and daughter
through undergraduate and graduate studies in the States. I was
his only offspring left behind in India. I expressed my desire to
seek higher education. He wanted me to start working. He was
getting on and didn't know how much longer he would be able to
work. BITS was a very expensive private college by Indian standards. My father bitched, Oh, I am tired of paying for your studies.
But I wanted to study further, as did a number of my batch mates
from BITS.

There were two avenues open to us. The first was of course
to go to the States for graduate study. The tuition and expenses
being prohibitive, one just had to get a scholarship from a university there. These were almost impossible to get. Only one or two
students in an entire batch of 600 from my college would get them.
In my sophomore year, I had been afflicted by a mystery illness
that had seen me lose my perch of being the straight topper of my
batch. No one could figure out what this mystery illness was. In
any case, I recovered after a few months.

The second option was to gain admission for an MBA to the Indian Institutes of Management (IIM) through a brutal competitive exam. An engineering degree with an MBA was a killer combination for a career in industry in India, as it's still today in India as well in as the US. I got admission into IIM Calcutta. My father, the same father who was demurring on my higher education, now encouraged me to join the institute. I also had won a scholarship to go to Purdue University in West Lafayette, Indiana for graduate study in engineering. My plan was to join the IIM, and apply for a US visa from Calcutta. If I got it, I would go to the States. If I didn't, I would stay back in Calcutta.

My father had western friends, especially many French, but whenever he would take his kids out in India with them for dinner, I was always the shy boy, slinking into a corner and never talking to the westerners. It was always my sister, being much more extroverted than me, who would perk up and talk to the foreigners. Even at age 21, I had never once talked to a white woman in my entire life.

The visa counselor at the US consulate in Calcutta was a blonde, blue-eyed, husky American woman. She summoned me to her window. I just couldn't stop looking at her brilliant blue eyes. They were electric blue. I remember her face as if it was yesterday. I had never seen eyes like that before. I stood transfixed. She said, this is such a good school, meaning IIM Calcutta, why do you want to leave it for Purdue? I could only mumble that Purdue was better, although later on in life I realized that that perhaps was not true. She once again emphasized how good and great IIM Calcutta was. I fumbled again, Purdue is better. Fed up of counseling me, she stamped my passport with the US visa.

My parents dropped me off at the airport in Delhi for the flight to the US. I didn't want to leave them. I had spent nine years living with them, most of them as their only child. We had become a very close-knit family. But I promised them that I would finish my master's degree in the States and then return to India. My brother was waiting in Chicago to pick me up and drive me down to Purdue. Everything in the States seemed to move super fast. The cars, the trucks, even the bicycles. The people were ginormous by Indian standards. I settled in Purdue in an apartment with three other Indian students.

I was determined to acculturate myself to American culture as soon as possible. The university had a host family program. I didn't know what it was, but signed up nevertheless. It would be nice to have a family in the US. My office mate, Rahil, was a Muslim from Pakistan who had finished his undergrad studies from the Arizona State University. He had enrolled in the host family program there. He told me that it was just a university-sponsored ruse to convert foreign students to Christianity. But I didn't care. I had already been exposed a lot to Christianity in India. It was not as if it was some evil thing. And then, in my mind, I was returning back to India after two years anyway. So how much would I get converted.

My host was my mailman. He had three young kids. We went out to the park one day with his wife and kids. One of my roommates had already spent a couple years in the States and was more worldly-wise than the rest of us. He was also very nosy. When my host came to visit me in our apartment the first time, my roommate poked him about his views about Islam. My host said that Americans didn't like it, that they feared that Muslims would come to the States and spread their faith. I tried to quickly paper over what was fast becoming a political discussion.

I had started eating beef as soon as I arrived in the States, but I had never had a steak before. One Friday, my host called me to his house in the country. He had another guest. She was from Hong Kong and was also attending Purdue. She seemed incredibly sophisticated to me. For dinner, there was steak and peas. The steak was blood-red. I took one bite of it and ran to the bathroom to throw up. I don't think anyone even noticed what had happened. I returned to the dining table and quietly finished my peas and left the remainder of the steak.

Life as a graduate student was very hectic. I spent almost all day and most evenings and nights in the laboratory growing semiconductor material. I would invariably miss lunch and often classes as well. My professor was a renowned professor, the only distinguished professor in the entire electrical engineering department. He was what was known in student parlance as a slave-driver. The minute I told any American student that Gunshor was my research advisor, my interlocutor would say, you have sold your soul. Sold my soul not in the religious sense, but in the sense that I had given my everything to the advisor, which was true in a way.

The stress of the job made my mystery illness flare up once again. Its onset was gradual, so even I didn't know what was going to hit me, until it really hit me. I stopped going to the department. I stopped going out. Near my apartment was a church. I had always meant to go in but I was too busy rushing to and fro from work to take out the time. Now I had the time as well as the inclination. I entered the church. I just wanted to meet the father (the pastor) and belt out my sob story and be cured and get back to work.

There was no one in the church. It stood at a prominent intersection. There was no Jesus on the cross inside the church, no Mother Mary. There was only a piano right in front of the church. Had I entered a conservatory by mistake? I had never been inside a church like this. Of course I could not pray to the piano. I hung around for a few minutes, said a silent prayer, and left.

Only much later I realized that I had entered a Protestant church. Christians make up some 3% of India's population, almost equally divided between Catholics and Protestants. But my exposure in India had only been to Catholicism. I thought that all Christian churches were like chapels or Catholic churches. That there would be a father in his white robes in front, and Jesus and Mary prominently displayed as well. In a Protestant church, the pastor was the equivalent of a father in a Catholic church. This was all a big learning process for me. I also learned that the US was a mostly Protestant country and that Protestantism had many denominations within itself. Many, many denominations. In Catholicism, as I had found rotating in my childhood from convent school to convent school, I had found little to no such distinctions.

My mailman host stuck by me through my travails. Every Sunday, I would go to church with him. It provided great succor to me. I was stuck between a very dominating brother and a very dominating professorial advisor. For some strange reason, my father and my brother believed that masturbation was the cause of my illness. They started obsessing over it. I wanted to tell them that no, I was not masturbating, but they did not seem to pay any attention. Masturbation in Indian households, as in many American ones, is a dirty word.

My brother would kick me out of bed sharp at 6 am and make me run six miles by the lake in Chicago (by this time I had moved in with him in Chicago to recover). Then I would return and make breakfast for him and for my dad (my dad was visiting from India). Then after a quick shower, I was booted out of the house to spend all day outside. All so that I couldn't masturbate indoors. It was a killing regimen. I found solace by spending a couple hours every day at a nearby church. I wouldn't tell my family though. They might have put an end to the practice.

My brother lived in the South Side of Chicago. Out there there was a Hindu center dedicated to Swami Vivekananda, the Hindu monk who had visited Chicago at the turn of the nineteenth century. I didn't want to go there, but my father insisted. He thought that meeting a Hindu spiritual leader would help me. But I was slowly becoming disconnected from Hinduism. I was only 22 and had already experienced much hardship in life. If a Hindu god was so kind and merciful as they made him out to be, why was he making a believer like me suffer so much?

And then there was still the mystery illness to cope with. I didn't drink, smoke, do drugs, even marijuana. I had never even had a girlfriend. Then why was God punishing me. No doctor could diagnose my ailment. This disease promised to be a lifelong affair. Would I be consigned to a looney-bin? My brother said that they would keep a nurse to keep guard over me all my life. I said, no, no, no, in my head. Nobody is watching over me all my life. I knew precisely what to do to end that.

My brother wanted me to stay on in the US, but I was scared and sick to my stomach. I wanted to return to the warmth and the comfort of the bosom that home was in India. I dare not tell my father and my brother that I was visiting a church regularly. They would fret that I was becoming Christian and ask me to cease and desist. In our household, only so much Christianity was allowed. A Bible, a picture of Jesus, a Christmas tree, that was about it.

My father and I flew back to India via France. On the French flight, a number of Jews were praying in the aisle. The flight stewardess scoffed that theirs was the only religious group allowed to behave like that. I had never met a Jewish person before. I didn't realize that they could be so orthodox. In Paris, my father took me to the obligatory nightclubs, the Moulin Rouge and the Folies Bergere. He was into that sort of thing. But my mind was elsewhere. I was not into French Can Can dance. My mind was fixated onto the future that awaited me in India.

In India they do not take it kindly if you return from the States for good. You must have done something really wrong to have been asked to leave the paradise that America was considered in India. And if you left the States without completing your degree, as I had, then that was akin to committing a capital crime. My mother met me on the front porch. She told me that I had brought shame to the family. That stung!

My mother was a big believer in Hindu *pujas* (worship). She was firmly convinced that one could expiate one's sins through Hindu rituals and chantings. But what sin had I committed? Again it all seemed to come down to my perceived practice of masturbation. My next-door cousin told my mother: If he had such a problem with masturbation, why did you let him go to a country like the US where there were so many beautiful white women? So the whole object of the *puja* was to rid me of the curse of masturbation.

My mother asked the local Hindu temple priest to come every day for 21 days for four hours a day to conduct the *puja*. I was to sit beside the priest on the carpet as he performed the rituals. I thought I would go mad. Twenty-one days, every day, for four hours every day. We sat down before the altar adorned with various Hindu deities. He chose one and started reciting verses in Sanskrit to it. I had to repeat each verse after him. I did not know Sanskrit. The meaning of not even a single word entered my head.

As I wrote earlier, there was also a picture of Christ on the altar. Christ had become my refuge. I kept reciting the Hindu phrases, but kept looking at Christ. Day after day passed. Finally the ordeal was over. Everybody thought that I was rid of the curse of masturbation. I felt that I was supposed to worship a Hindu god but instead I had come much closer to Christ. He had helped me get through the ordeal. My heart had become one with His. I slept in the same living room every night, right under the altar. I started praying to Christ when I went to bed and when I got up. My conversion was not yet complete. That would take some more time. And I daren't tell anyone at home what was swirling through my heart and mind. It would have to remain my own little secret. If my mother found out, she would try to talk me out of my heart change or even set up another 21-day *puja*. I was having none of that. My butt ached from sitting on the floor for so long.

CHAPTER 4

Tough Years in India

It was always going to be tough, but I never realized that it would be this tough. I had entered Purdue's PhD program at age 21. Had I completed it in four or five years, at age 25 or 26, I would have been among the very young PhDs in the United States. A professorship at a major university would not have been far away. I would have become the apple of the eye of my family (although in my mom's eye that laurel would always remain with my older brother). But now I was 22, back in India, a shame on my family, with no job or any other prospects. Yes, I had a master's and a bachelor's degree from a premier Indian college, but once you were out of school, jobs were scarce. Additionally, in 1991, the year I returned to India, the country went bankrupt and had to undertake a major overhaul of its economy, which made corporate hiring even more difficult. Employers would look askance if I told them what had happened to me at Purdue. And if I didn't tell them about my stint there, they would ask what I had done a whole year right after college. Saying that I had taken a whole year off to visit my brother in America would not have cut it. Who in India took a year off to gallivant in America.

My next-door cousin and his wife came to visit my parents and me. My cousin ran a metal-working factory, in which I had spent time during my college days. It was tough work. My cousin was a genius at shaping sheet metal into all kinds of forms. He was a mechanical engineer. I was an electrical engineer, so much of the work at the factory was novel for me. My cousin asked me what I wanted to do. I replied that I wanted to start my own business. He said why don't you start coming to my factory starting the very next day. The following day, sharp at 8 am, I climbed into my cousin's car to go to his factory.

Once I reached the factory, I decided that I would work like a normal laborer there. Most of the labor was from the country of Nepal. They were tough, hardened men. The factory was cramped and quite a dangerous place. If you took your eye off the ball, you might lose a finger to a machine. I wanted to do all the tough jobs but my cousin refrained me from doing so. He was scared that I would hurt myself. At lunch, all his entrepreneur friends would gather at his shop. We would order some delicious Indian food— often chicken tikka masala and garlic naan—and banter around. It was the happiest time of my life in Delhi.

One day, two successful businessmen, both brothers, came to my cousin's shop. They asked me what I did. I told them that I had returned from Purdue. They were appalled that I had left such an acclaimed university as Purdue to work in what was basically a sweatshop. They urged me to go back. But there was that mystery illness. I never knew when it would strike again. Since everyone assumed that masturbation was the cause of my disease, I too had started believing it. One day, I took a while in the bathroom and my cousin me that that the factory was a sacred place for him and dare I not masturbate in there. I took the insult in my stride.

Spiritually these were lost years for me. My mother used to go to a religious service, which was primarily Hindu in nature, but also drew from Buddhist and Christian traditions. It is very fashionable for elite Hindus in India to go Buddhist. What they don't realize is that most of the precepts that Buddha taught like reincarnation and meditation were taken by him from Hinduism when he founded his new faith. So the Hindu elite thinks that it's learning something new, but actually it isn't, it's all there in their own religion.

The service was held in the mansion of a billionaire in one of the most posh neighborhoods of Delhi. Mostly the rich and the powerful would come to the service. It really wasn't a service at all. It was a hangout for Delhi's glitterati to attempt their hand at spirituality while having tea and delicious scones. Dark skin is a sin in India just like it is in the US. My mother is dark, not very dark but wheatish, what they call in India after the color of wheat. I too am of the similar color. Most of India's glitterati is fair in color. It is important to be fair in India. Fair skin garners one immediate respect. Most of the women who used to come to the service were middle-aged and fat. My mother's brother's wife, Therese, was French, and lived in India. Therese would always tell my mother that Indian women fell apart after marriage, that is they lost shape and gained weight. Until marriage, many Indian girls remain slim. Marriage offers a strange sense of security to them. Divorce is still a big stigma in India. So the women forget about their figure and go on an eating spree once married. Strenuous exercise is out. In most cases, their husbands too are falling apart. You can imagine then that any physical intimacy becomes like elephants wrestling in mud.

But Indian women who are fair take great pride in their skin even if they have fallen apart. And then the richie rich women who came to the service came in fancy cars all driven by chauffeurs. I would show up in a beat-up scooter. Yes, my English was very good, but my skin was dark. Some of the women thought that I came to eye them. That was a joke because I find fat women, fair or dark, repulsive. I was told not to attend the service anymore. I came to realize the tremendous amount of class distinctions that existed among Hindus even when it came to religion. They were not able to tolerate a young man of 23 who came to their place to clear his head and seek some spiritual solace.

I took up a job. As is common in India, I was promised something and paid something else. I was offered $1,000 a month when I signed up, but my first pay check showed only $750. The company was run by Sikhs and Hindus. I was having some issues at work, and my mother counseled me to speak to a Mrs. Khanna from her religious service. Khanna was a rich, fat Hindu woman. At that time, my brother was doing very well professionally in the States. Khanna gave me some advice, but started by saying that there was once a Mary who had two sons, one who was doing much better than the other and who the Mary was partial to. The Mary that she was referring to was my mother. Mary is a common name for a Christian maidservant in India. They are typically dark because they have converted from the untouchable caste of Hinduism. Caste Hindus still look down upon them even after they have converted to Christianity. So all these fair maidens in the religious service called my mother Mary behind her back just because she was dark and not very rich. Now the name-calling was not just being done behind my ma's back. It was being done openly to the face of her son.

My mother held the highest regard for Khanna and this was how that fat ogre spoke about her. I felt humiliated but I didn't bring the matter up with my mother. I didn't want her to feel miserable. But I think it was that talk more than any other event in my life that turned me away from Hinduism. These people who claimed to be virtuous Hindus practiced discrimination at all levels. Yes, we were not obscenely rich, but we were a respectable middle-class family. My father was a veteran who had fought three wars gloriously for his nation. Unlike the US, veterans are given very little importance in India. I am sure that a thousand years ago, when Muslims conquered India, Hindus even then too were wallowing in their caste system and in the mistreatment of their soldiers. That's why India had to go under the yoke of first Islamic rule, and then British rule, for a thousand years.

Yet caste Hindus in India seem to have learned nothing from their own millennium-long ordeal. They still keep beating up on the untouchable caste, but when the untouchable caste decides to convert to Christianity, they go ballistic. There are about 200 million untouchables in India. Many, if not most, would like to convert to Christianity and escape the hugely oppressive Hindu system of caste that they find themselves entrapped in. There are government affirmative action programs for the untouchable caste but only as long as it stays Hindu. If untouchables convert to Christianity they lose those rights. The Indian government has officially stepped in to dissuade conversions, even though the right to proselytize is enshrined in the Indian Constitution. The Indian government is bound to uphold the Indian Constitution, but it behaves otherwise when it comes to proselytizing Christianity to the untouchables of India. I guess that there are workarounds for everything in life. Why doesn't the Indian government in one fell full stroke strike down the abominable Hindu caste system?

In 1993, I won a Rotary scholarship to go to England for two months to mix and mingle with the locals there. It was a much-needed reprieve from the heat and dust of India. We were a team of four young professionals led by a middle-aged businessman called Singh. He was a Sikh. I had been chosen as the number one pick. But Singh soon realized that I was quite poor. In addition I was the darkest of the lot. He was a rich man, and expected due deference from his team. Two of team-members referred to him reverentially as Singh *Saab*. *Saab* can be connoted to mean anywhere between calling someone a lord or sir. Another member and I thought that it was too demeaning to use the term. We addressed Singh as Mr. Singh, which he didn't like at all.

The other recalcitrant member was a major TV personality in India, so Singh couldn't do anything to him. But he reserved his ire for me at any and all times. Luckily, I became quite popular with many of the Brits that we met there. I tried to steer clear of Singh as much as possible. Our schedule would include visits to many famous cathedrals in England. They were uniformly gob-smackingly beautiful. I didn't have much change to spare but made sure to light a candle in each church and put some money in the donation box. I felt very much at peace inside the cathedrals.

I guess most of them were Anglican churches that we went to. They unfailingly had Christ on the cross and images of Mary. This was what I was used to worshipping at my convent schools in India. The cathedral visits really allowed me to tolerate Singh and go through a journey that he was making rotten for me. Still, I never addressed him as *Saab*, much to his consternation.

After the official visit to England was over, I decided to buy a Eurail train ticket and travel around Europe for two weeks. I went to Paris where I made sure to pay obeisance at the Notre Dame and the Sacre Coeur. I went to Salzburg, where I took the *Sound of Music* bus tour and then went to see Hitler's Eagle's Nest in Obersalzberg. Salzburg was a magical city, with people playing music on the street even at 2 am. I noticed a poster for yoga and instantly felt at home. My budget was very tight. I lived on pizza slices and stayed in youth hostels. Often I would arrive at a hostel when it was closed and just leave my baggage in the lobby without a care in the world. I found Europe to be, for lack of a better word, much more honest than India. I was quite confident that no one would pinch my luggage in Europe and no one ever did. In India, I would dare not leave my stuff unattended by trustworthy eyes.

Wherever in Europe I got the chance to visit a cathedral or a church, I would do so and pray. I would pray for myself but also for my entire family—my father, my mother, my brother and his family, and my sister and her family. I don't remember asking God for anything. It was just a moment of silent communion for me, and for thanking the LORD for having given me the opportunity to have had such a magical tour of Europe. Often I would sleep on the train to save on paying for lodging. Eurail allowed you to travel unlimited for a set number of days. So if I had to go from Frankfurt to Salzburg, I would take the train to Vienna, disembark and then take another train to Salzburg. The detour allowed me to spend the night on the train without paying anything extra.

I had some business to transact in Germany, after which I flew home to India. The Germans had offered me an agency to sell their products in India, and I duly got going. They then wanted me to manufacture their products in India. But I had neither the land and building nor any capital. Most people who I approached in India to become a partner wanted to shove me out of the project. The concept of sweat equity did not exist in India then. It was terribly frustrating. I had spent four years trying to attract a major German company to India, but when the time came, I could not make things happen. My father tried his best to help, but he too had limited resources. He decided to sell one of his properties to fund my business, but I refrained him from doing so because the property did not belong to me.

I was running around like a chicken with my head cut off to make the project take off. One day, at the peak of summer, I rode my scooter about 100 miles in 120 degrees weather. The visor of my helmet was broken, so all the hot air just steamed in through to my face. Noel Coward wrote that only mad dogs and English-men go out in the midday sun in India, but I swear to God, that day I saw no Englishmen anywhere and only one pye-dog (stray dog). All I remember was the *loo* (Indian summer wind) blowing around and a red haze enveloping everything. There was not a soul to be found on the streets.

Despite my frantic efforts, I could not make the German project take off. A much bigger Indian company grabbed it hook, line and sinker and decided that I would have no part in it. I was completely deflated. After Purdue, this was the second major opportunity gone awry in my life. Then once again the mystery illness appeared. This time it was really bad. My sleep cycle got reversed. It was 1995. The OJ Simpson trial was shown live on TV in India, but because of the time difference between America and India, it came on at an unearthly hour. I used to watch the trial all night and go to sleep all day.

My poor mom, she really looked after me all this while. She carted me to all kinds of doctors, but they could not figure out my ailment. My father took me to a US-returned Indian doctor and insisted that masturbation was my problem. The doctor was aghast. He drew a picture of the male organs and told me to enjoy masturbation. Now it was the turn of my father to be aghast. He had grown up in the British Raj in India and read a number of Victorian books, all of which derided masturbation as "self-abuse," a practice that destroyed one's self. Since my father kept insisting to the doctor that I had a problem, the doctor prescribed me a cocktail of drugs.

I took it and went crazy and ingested a chemical. I was taken to a hospital where I was declared safe. The following day my friend called the doctor and asked him why he had done what he had done. The doctor replied nonchalantly that he wanted to experiment on me. My friend was furious. He wanted to go and break the windows of the doctor's car. I told him to cool it. My mother was at her wit's end. She did not know what would become of me. Finally someone in her religious service suggested a doctor. After my experience with the drug cocktail, I was hellbent on not taking more medication. Still I accompanied my mother to the doctor. Sometimes I would refuse to go, and my mother would go all alone to keep the doctor's appointment. I have never forgotten the succor my mother provided me in 1995, and have always tried to repay my debt to for her for it.

The doctor's name was John Lal. By name, the doctor appeared Christian. Many Indian Christians retain their Hindu last names. He immediately recognized my problem as bipolar disorder. In India, it is impolite to ask a person's faith, but I was convinced that the man was Christian. He told my mother that I was depressed and that he needed to bring me to a stable state before he could administer the right medication to me. Since I point-blank refused to take any medication, my mother mixed the anti-depressant in my lemonade and served it to me surreptitiously. I recovered in a couple of months and then the doctor prescribed me the medication for bipolar disorder. By now my resistance to medication had melted away.

Dr. John Lal was a man sent from God. I am firmly convinced that Christ sent him for me. The medication worked like magic. Dr. Lal said that if the symptoms of my illness did not reappear in two years, I would probably not get an episode of bipolar again, and if they did not appear in ten years, I would never get an episode again. For the first two years, I would mark off every day in my calendar. I healed perfectly. Christ is the ultimate healer. Christ came in the form of Dr. Lal to heal me. It is 25 years now and I haven't had an episode of bipolar again. Just as soon as I was recovering, my mother spoke to an Alcoholics Anonymous person to send my dad into alcohol rehab.

I was dead-set against sending my dad anywhere but my next-door cousin counseled that just as obesity had set in in India, so too had weight-loss centers emerged to counter it. It was the same with alcohol rehab programs, he said. I knew nothing about what kind of alcohol rehab program my father was being sent to, but I agreed, albeit reluctantly. Later on I discovered that it was a just a couple of thugs jailing patients and administering sound thrashings to them if they tried to leave. It was a pure money-making racket. Around the same time, my mother broke her hip. My assistant and I were working on my business, and my mother wanted my assistant to drive her to the grocery market. A grocery market in India is a virtual pell-mell. There are vegetable vendors all displaying their wares on the road, there are people, there are cars, there are scooters, there are cycle rickshaws. I told my mom that I would be done with my assistant in a while and then she could have him, but she refused to wait and hailed a cycle rickshaw to go to the market.

Cycle rickshaws in India then were very unstable. They had three high wheels and an open platform at the back to sit on, from where one could fall off very easily. Now, twenty-five years later, they have been made more safe by providing a mandatory cover for them. In any event, there was a scooter whizzing around in the market. He hit my mother's rickshaw and knocked her down. I received a phone call from the market to come pick up my mother at once. She was writhing in excruciating pain. I immediately de-cided to rush her to the military hospital. My mother was cursing at me and blaming me for her accident and her pain. But I ignored all her utterances. I had to get her healed. The doctors did an X-ray on her and said that she had broken her hip and had to have hip replacement surgery.

Now both my father and mother were in hospital. I used to visit my father every week taking fruits and sweets with me, and I was by the side of my mother the rest of the time. I know now that only Christ gave me the strength to endure this time. My father was a military veteran, so my mother was admitted to the ward meant for the wives of military officers who had retired from service.

There were about 20 women jam-packed in one room. Serving officers and their families got the best treatment, then military vets, and then the families of the vets. Such was the pecking order in the hospital, which actually meant that the wives of vets received little to no service.

Nobody came to pick up their waste. I took upon myself the task of cleaning the women's waste matter. One woman hailed me as a Florence Nightingale to my mother. I would carry women on stretchers and board them into ambulances. It was the happiest time of my life. I felt that I was doing the LORD's work, Christ's work. I received so much adulation, so much love, so much gratitude from the women that I remember it to this day. My father had a Bible on his bookshelf. I opened it to read it to derive some solace in this hour of extreme need, but I got confused. In any case, I read the Sermon on the Mount, which lifted me greatly. The sermon was also one of Mahatma Gandhi's favorite scriptures. I had read it in school and keep rereading it almost every day now. It held me together during all those very trying months.

The time came for my mother's hip operation. I was supposed to donate blood for it since the hospital had a blood for blood policy. My aunt told me not to donate blood. She was worried if I fell sick from giving blood, who would look after my mother and my father. I approached the surgeon asking him if I could get blood donated by someone else. He was an ace surgeon, a Colonel who had the reputation of being a martinet. He was retiring soon and my mom's operation would be the last that he would be performing. I had never given blood before. A hip replacement surgery requires an enormous amount of blood. I was scared. The doctor saw through my fear. But he said that the hospital would not accept the blood of a cycle rickshaw driver. I had to be the one giving blood.

The nurse inserted the needle. And then she kept sucking out packets and packets of blood. It seemed like an endless flow. I fainted. Finally she had had enough. It was like Dracula sucking all the blood out of me. But it was for a good cause. After the operation, the doctor hailed me and told me that it had gone fine. I was extremely grateful to him. Recovery in the hospital took more than a month. I brought my mother home. She was cantankerous, still blaming me for her accident. She still holds that over me and will hold it against me until she dies. That obstinacy is because even though she realizes that Christ was a prophet, she has still not accepted Him as her true LORD and Savior, her only one and only LORD and Savior. She is still lost in the obscurantism of Hinduism. So be it.

News came from the alcohol rehab center that my father had escaped. My mother was insistent that he continue with his rehab. She wanted to soak him dry. The rehab thugs discovered that my father was staying at the army officer's club. They asked me to drive them there. As soon as my father had had his dinner, they waylaid him and put him in the back seat of the car. I was driving. The two thugs were in the back with my father. My father was 65, but still quite strong. He put up a stiff fight. The thugs kept bashing him. I told them to stop otherwise I would pull over. We were on the highway now. Indian highways are a melee of cars, trucks, three-wheelers, two-wheelers, donkey-carts, camels, you name it, it's all there. Traffic moves barely at 30 mph.

My father had a shock of white hair and fair skin. White women visiting India are always susceptible to getting raped. This was 1996, way before the days of cell phones in India. There were no landlines on the highways either. But ever so often, there was a police checkpoint. The next thing I knew, a cop accosted me at a checkpoint. Apparently someone had alerted the cops that a white woman (who in effect was my dad) was being raped in a car. Rape is of course a serious matter. We were carted to the next police station. The officer on duty heard me out and decided to release us. Then my father called his brother, who was a lawyer. He threatened the cop with a law suit. The cop told me that I had made his night hell and quickly recanted. My father was free to go his sweet way. Obviously the denouement didn't go too well with the thugs, who were in it only for the money, or with my mother, who, Jesus bless her soul, at heart only had the good of my dad.

My brother came from America for a visit and promised my mother that he would take me to the States and loan me half a million dollars to start my own business there. That of course never came to pass. But he invited me to visit the US and stay with him over the summer. He had just had a baby and I was eager to see my little nephew. Since I had been to the US before, and had returned to India thereby proving to the visa authorities that I would not disappear in the States, getting a US tourist visa was a breeze. My father returned home and started living separately from my mother. But I knew that they would kiss and make up at some point, so I was confident that I could leave them alone in India, while I went gallivanting to the States. I was so glad for the break. It had been a traumatic year: first my illness, then my dad's, and finally my mom's. But I made it through it with the grace of the LORD, Jesus Christ. Never Give Up. I saw this emblazoned on a church in America many years later. Yes, sir, Never Give Up. The LORD is always with you. But never give up. He is the one who instills in one the courage to never give up. One is but putty in His hands. But one must allow oneself to be made putty. That is what devotion is all about, that is what submission is all about, that is what prayer is all about.

My father had a love of foreign languages, and because he realized in the beginning of 1996 that my health was still delicate and that I was not working full-time, he asked me to enroll for German classes at Delhi's Goethe Institute (also called the Max Mueller Bhavan (house in Hindi) after a famous German scholar who had studied Sanskrit and the Hindu scriptures). The classes were in the afternoon, five days a week, three hours a day. When my parents fell sick, going to German class would become a refuge for me. Even though the course was introductory, it lasted for six months, by the end of which one was supposed to have acquired intermediate proficiency in German.

We were about 10 students in class. There was a tall, good-looking girl called Aditi who I was really attracted to. We used to sit at the back of the room and make jokes all class long. The funny thing was that in school and college I had always been a front-bencher but now I was enjoying being a back-bencher. Aditi came from a rich, privileged background. A chauffeur would drive her to class every day. I would come to class in my two-wheeler or sometimes in my dad's Fiat car. Class matters a lot in India. We would get about a half-hour break so there was plenty of time to mix and mingle with one another. One day the whole class decided to go and see the film, *Philadelphia*, which starred Denzel Washington. The classmate seated next to me ran a small hotel in a shabby part of town. He had never been outside India, although I suspect much of the clientele at his hotel were cheap hippy-type foreign tourists.

Suddenly in the middle of the movie, he piped up, blacks are a very warm people, whites are cold. I couldn't fathom where he got that from although I could relate to what he said given the year that I had spent in the Midwest in 1990–91. One girl in class seemed to have taken a shine to me. She called me at my home and pleaded that if I didn't go out with her, she would commit suicide. She said that without coming close to me, she couldn't eat food, she couldn't sleep. I was 27. Other than my mother's and my sister's hands, I had never ever touched the hands of a woman before. I was not attracted to the woman. Plus I had morals. I was not planning to sleep with a woman before marriage. A couple of my classmates urged me to do her but I resisted the temptation. In any case, since I was leaving for the US in the summer, I was not reenrolling in German classes again, so I would not have to spend more time with her.

I had planned to spend a couple weeks in Germany trying to find a new partner for my business. My old partner simply refused to meet me. I travelled the length and breadth of Germany in the beautiful Deutsche Bahn. Germany is a country with a lot of peculiar, unique customs. Germans consider a four-hour train ride in their country very taxing. A four-hour train ride in India, and even in the US, is considered piffling. I boarded the train from Frankfurt to Munich, which is about a four hour-ride. My host met me at Munich station and expectantly inquired if I was not tired from my exhausting journey. Expectantly because he expected me to say yes. I said no.

It was a Friday. Friday afternoons is time for *feierabend* in Germany—time to go home and relax for the weekend. My business counterpart was in no mood for work. He pointed to a five-star hotel and asked if I wanted to stay there for the weekend. I gulped! I didn't know whether he was volunteering to pay for my stay or not. At that time, I was too bashful to ask. Now I would have done it without a second's hesitation. I was on a budget and scared that I might expend a lot of money on the hotel if my business counterpart didn't pony up the tab. So I said no to the hotel and asked the manager to have the meeting on Friday itself. There was no one in his office building except for the two of us. The manager was in no mood to transact any business. He ended up telling me all about his family. Nothing came out of the visit to Munich.

I then made my way to Stuttgart, near where I had to meet a manager in a cute town called Hechingen Stetten. It is one of the prettiest places I have ever visited. My business counterpart was late. I was very hungry and very thirsty. The pension was just as I had imagined a German pension to be. A homely hostess, cute rooms, a beautiful picture of someone imbibing a Coca Cola on the wall. I was desperate for a drink. My hostess brought me a Coke. It felt like the sweetest drink that I had ever had. I would not eat anything even though the hostess insisted. I wanted to wait for my business counterpart. When he arrived, the hostess told him that I had waited four hours for him without eating anything and almost drinking nothing. He was touched. We formed a real bond, although businesswise nothing fructified. I left. I slept on the train often, cleaned up and shaved on it, went all over Germany in search for business, but nothing realized. Even with a new German partner, I knew it would take me three years to build their brand in India. And then when the time came up to set up a manufacturing facility, I would not have the money to do so. It was all going to be déjà-vu. But without a partner, I was completely dead in the water. It was all very deflating. With a heavy heart, I boarded the flight to the US.

The flight was magical. The soccer Euro Cup final was on between Germany and Croatia. I didn't realize how much Germans loved the game until I was on the flight. All the flight stewardesses were constantly getting score updates from the pilots up in front. And then I spoke to the chief stewardess in German. She told all her crew, he speaks German, give him the best treatment. Suddenly I was being wowed by delicious treats from first class. I was still seated in economy class. All around me the economy-class passengers wondered what had I done to deserve this welcome. And what had they done to deserve the scrimpy fare that had become their lot. I realized then how much Germans loved their language and how much they appreciated anyone who spoke it.

Growing up in an Anglo-environment in India, this is a rare feeling if one encounters an Anglo like a Brit or an American. The US makes all Indians write a ridiculously easy (for many Indians) test of English as a foreign language to get into an American university. After twenty-five years of living in an Anglo-culture (in the US and partly in the UK), I have come to realize how much Anglos (the Americans and the Brits) take people speaking English for granted. I suspect that 300 years of world domination, the first two hundred years by the Brits and the last hundred by the Americans, makes them expect everyone to speak English. And if a non-native English speaker, especially a colored one, speaks it better than them, that just makes them hate her for it. A colored person gets no brownie points, or even affection or admiration, in America for speaking better English than an American. I think Anglos should take the Savior's message of humility to heart and rectify their misbehavior. Hubris is not good. Arrogance only takes you away from God.

CHAPTER 5

Illinois and France

M y older brother was present at JFK airport in New York City to receive me. He drove a luxury car. He had done well for himself in America. He adored it. Like me, he too had had a Christian education in India. I remember one of his schools was called Christ the King. Christ truly is King, isn't he? My brother worked in New York City and lived in Parsippany, New Jersey. He lived about an hour's drive from work. I was excited to see my little nephew and my sister-in-law. She had spent a year with me in my parents' house before she got the visa to come to the US, and I had really not got to know her very well in India. That would change now and how.

I couldn't drive in the US because I didn't have a license. I didn't even have an international driver license, although I am unsure how valid it is in the US. In any case, in India we follow the British custom and drive on the left side of the road. Without practice of driving in American conditions, it could be dangerous driving in the US. But I couldn't sit all alone all day in my brother's one-bedroom apartment. My brother was a member of a squash club in New Jersey called the Chatham Club. I had played squash at a high level in India. I wanted to continue doing so in the US. To get to the club by bus, I would have to board a bus from Parsippany to Morristown, where I would take the transfer to Chatham. Then I would walk about two miles to reach the club.

I would be up at 7 am and be sure to leave home quietly without disturbing anybody. I wouldn't have any breakfast nor did I carry any food with me. On the bus one day, an African American woman told me, Thank God you are Indian and not Chinese; the Chinese have no religion. I wanted to tell her, but refrained, that we are all children of the same God and that Christ is the LORD and Savior of all of us. Sometimes a kind soul driving to the club would notice my squash bag and give me a ride until there, but more often than not, I would have to walk. Whenever anybody offered me a ride, I would think how kind Americans were. But later I had the same experience in France and other parts of the world. As I said, we are all children of the same God and Jesus is our LORD and Savior. He didn't make any of his people anywhere anymore special than any other people of His.

I would reach the club around 9 am. The squash pro there realized how good I was and instead of busting his butt playing with club members, made me play with them. Squash is an incredibly demanding sport. I would play until around 1pm, after which I would make the trek back home. By the time I reached there, I would be ravenous. My brother would be at his office and my sister-in-law with her baby in the apartment. My sister-in-law taught me a number of Indian dishes to cook. We became firm friends and would often go for a drive together. New Jersey in the fall is simply beautiful. My brother was a difficult, domineering husband, so my sister-in-law would confide in me. I suspect that my brother felt that we were scheming behind his back, but that was not the case. I just felt a moral obligation to be by my sister-in-law's side because she had married into our family and because my brother was mistreating her.

I knew that there was no future for me back in India. My sister-in-law advised me that if I wanted to stay back in the US, I could only do so as a student. I started looking at MBA schools in New York, the two main ones being Columbia and New York University. I went to attend an admission session at Columbia.

They put me in touch with a professor there. I had already taken the GMAT—the Graduate Management Admission Test—which is used to evaluate candidates for MBA programs. My score in it was truly astronomical. As soon as the professor learned my score, he said just apply, I will get you in. The problem though was the steep cost of admission. Tuition at Columbia or NYU for a two-year MBA program could cost north of a hundred thousand dollars, even then, twenty-five years ago. My father could have rustled up a small portion of the money, but I had no money of my own. I confided my situation to my sister-in-law. I didn't have a green card nor was I a US citizen, so I couldn't avail myself of government student loans. I never expected my sister-in-law to tell my brother about my plans, but she did.

The three of us went out to a Thai restaurant for dinner. Because her baby was crying, my sister-in-law had to rush back home. The next 45 minutes were among the most difficult of my life. My brother raked me over the coals. He told me not to expect a penny from him. He said that his family would only grow, and that he wouldn't be able to help me out with even a cent. He scalded me. I felt small, degraded. I just prayed to Jesus silently during all the time that my brother barked at me. He had forgotten all about the half-a-million dollar business loan that he had promised my mother in India that he would give me in the States. He basically wanted me to spend some weeks with him in the US and then get the hell back to India.

I had bought a few air tickets called VUSA—Visit USA—to travel around the US. My brother was keeping tabs on exactly where I was going. I told him that I was going to Florida to see the theme parks there. Instead, I flew to Urbana-Champaign in Illinois, where my college mate from India had done his MBA from the University of Illinois. My friend took me to the general engineering department where I was immediately granted admission into the master's program and a teaching assistantship. Illinois is the heart of the American heartland. Most of the professors are sturdy, kindly Christian folk. Not so the head of the department of general engineering. He wanted to interview me before finalizing my appointment. Everything was going swimmingly well. I had not mentioned Purdue in my application for admission because I had been there less than a year and because I had not earned a degree from there. Many college applications only ask you to mention colleges that you have attended for a year or more. To bolster my credentials, I unnecessarily told the head that I had been at Purdue. He went ballistic. He asked why I had not mentioned it in my application. I explained why. But he wouldn't accept my explanation and rescinded my admission and assistantship.

That was a grievous blow. Attending Illinois was the only way I could stay on in the States and build a new life. I asked the head that if his concern was that I had done something unethical at Purdue, I would get a certificate from there to prove that I hadn't. He still wouldn't budge. Nevertheless I drove to down to Purdue with a couple friends. The drive through the corn fields in the month of August was magical. All of the corn plants were turning colorful and the corn ripe to be plucked. At Purdue, I met a professor, Prof. Gray, with whom I had taken a course. He told me that I had cleared my master's thesis at Purdue and had almost completed two courses. I had only four more courses left to get a master's degree from Purdue. That would take me just a year. Why didn't I return back to Purdue?

Gray was a lovely, kindly man. But I told him that I had had such a horrendous time at Purdue that I just couldn't fathom returning to that campus. Everything there held unhappy memories for me. So he gave me a letter stating that I had had done nothing unethical whatsoever at Purdue, which I promptly handed to the head of the general engineering department at Illinois. He still wouldn't change his stance. Numerous professors approached him on my behalf, but he wouldn't listen. I would wear the same suit to the department every day and carry a leather briefcase. The deputy head of the department holed me up. He said that I see you come here day after day with the same briefcase. He said that they didn't want to have a smart, persistent student like me fall through the cracks. He said that he would broach my case to his boss. But the head still wouldn't move.

I was determined to stay on in Illinois. My undergraduate degrees were in electrical engineering and in physics. I decided that I would try every possible department to get admission into. An Indian professor in mechanical engineering offered me admission and an assistantship. But his student cautioned me that it would take three years to get a master's degree with him. The norm for a master's degree was two years, sometimes faster. I spoke French and German. I had decided that I would even approach the language departments in order to stay on at Illinois.

It had been more than a week at Illinois. My brother in New Jersey was getting antsy. Where was I? I should have returned to New Jersey by then. He felt that I was up to no good and made his sentiments clear to my sister-in-law. But I was out of the dictatorial reach of my brother's. That in itself was a big relief. In any case, I had much bigger fish to fry at Illinois. One day, I knocked on the door of a professor in the general engineering department and asked to use her office phone. I called the associate head of the electrical engineering department, NN Rao. He told me to visit him the following day.

I went to meet him. He took one look at my GPA, where I went to school in India, and my GRE (Graduate Record Examinations) scores and told me that I was admitted forthwith into the electrical engineering department. I almost died with relief. He asked me to find a professor to fund my studies. But professors were crawling the hallways looking for students to fund and do their research for them. I quickly signed up with a professor. My deal was done. I would be staying on in the US. I didn't even call my tyrannical brother to tell him anything. Let him stew in suspense. My sister-in-law must have told him that I was seeking admission to a school.

Because I was on a tourist visa, I had to fly to Canada or Mexico and return back to the US with the appropriate student visa. The foreign student counselor at Illinois was a beautiful, Christian woman. I would have proposed to her right away except that she already had a ring on her finger.

I flew to Toronto one week to meet an old business friend. He showed me the CN Tower. I hesitated to walk over the glass floor at the very top. In my hotel, at the bar, I was approached by a young woman. She was a hooker. I tried to convince her to leave her profession, but she said that it was quite lucrative. In any case, I was not going to do anything further with her. Christian education in India had imbibed in me too many morals, most of all to resist devilish temptations of the flesh. On Friday of that week, I returned to Toronto airport to fly back to the US. I stood in line to get my visa stamped. The officer on duty told me to go to a nearby table to fill out a form.

I should have returned back to the same officer. Christ was urging me to do so. The officer had already cleared me but for the formality of obtaining the form. My Christian instinct told me to just dawdle before her counter opened up again. Buy I refuted my impulse and went to the next open officer. He took one look at my application and refused to give me a visa. Ever since, I have been determined to follow my Christian instinct. Christ is there to guide us at all the crossroads of life, and navigate the lanes and bylanes of this complex world, if only we are willing to listen to Him. First we must purify our souls and come close to Him. Then we must keep our ear out to listen to Him. He is not just a spiritual being out there to sort out our spiritual complexities. He guides us, and how, in the temporal world as well.

I was stuck in Toronto now with little money. I called up my foreign student counselor, who had given me her home number. She was dumbstruck why I was facing trouble getting back into the States. She reiterated that what I was attempting was only a routine procedure, which many students before me had undertaken. In any case, I had nothing to do but while the weekend away at a billiards hall. The owner was Indian. He said that he could hook me up with one of his waitresses. I refused. Monday came and I was there at the US embassy at the crack of down to get my visa. There they told me to go back to the airport. At the airport once again an officer refused my case and asked me to wait in a room.

I must have waited for four hours. I missed my flight. I told the officers that I had missed my flight, but they didn't seem to care. I don't know why immigration officers make you wait so long. They either must be very busy or they just want to show you your place. I suspect that it's the latter. Finally I was summoned. The officers told me that because I was attending the University of Chicago, they were letting me back into the States. Actually, I was not going to the University of Chicago, but the University of Illinois. Chicago is a private school and considered more prestigious than Illinois. But this time I let my Christian instinct guide me and kept my loud mouth shut. I let them believe I was attending Chicago. The LORD knows when and how to guide us. He wroughts such miracles in our lives. We should open our eyes and be able to recognize them. I called my foreign student counselor. She was delirious!

Coming back into the States was such a relief. The immigration officers in Toronto had told me that had they denied me the visa, I would have had to return to India and apply for a US visa from there. Wow, that would have been a long detour. Toronto to Chicago, versus Toronto to somewhere in Europe and then to India, where if I had been lucky enough to get the US visa, the return trek back to Chicago. I had no money for all of this round-the-world trip. I was a starving student. Particularly since I was not getting paid anything by the university until I converted the tourist visa into a student one. For three months, my thousand dollar a month salary had been accumulating with the university. Now when I came back to Illinois I received the ginormous sum of three thousand dollars. It felt so sweet! I lived in the dorm in my own room but shared the bathroom with another guy. We trusted one another so much that we left our respective bathroom doors unlocked. My roommate was Arabic. He had a white girlfriend. I went to the ATM one day to withdraw money. There was no money left in my bank account. I was dumbfounded! There should have at least been three thousand dollars in there. I spoke to the bank manager. He said that he would investigate. Prior to trying to obtain the money at Illinois, I had spent the month-long winter break at my brother's in New Jersey.

45

During that period, ATM cameras showed a Middle Eastern-looking man showing up in a white sports car day after day and withdrawing money from my ATM account. I didn't complain against my Arabic roommate to the cops. I had no proof against him. The guy withdrawing money didn't look like him, although it could have been one of his friends. My Christian reticence prevented me from accusing someone against whom I had no evidence. But the cops insisted on interrogating him. He became mad at me. Finally, a cop summoned me. He said that they had much bigger fish to fry like rape cases and gun shootings and would not be able to devote time to a piffling of a case like mine. I was deflated. I lost all my money because the time period to elapse a complaint with the bank had lapsed. Local lawyers warned me not to take the bank to court. They said that my bank was a big deal in small towns like Urbana and Champaign, and it would have made sure to have had all of the area's legal firms on its rolls so that it couldn't be sued. Wow! I was learning some neat things about America. America was founded on Christian principles of right and wrong and look how people have twisted them so much.

I lost a of my money and had to build my nest egg up. Even though I only received just over a thousand dollars a month, by living sparsely, by not smoking, by not drinking, by not doing drugs, by not womanizing, by leading a clean Christian life, I was easily able to save about 25% of that income. My father had taught me French as a kid and imbided in me a love for French culture. I always wanted to live in France. Lo and behold! One day there was a flyer advertizing a two-semester work-study program at France's premier college, the Ecole Polytechnique in Paris. I talked to my French friends about it and they insisted that I must apply.

I was invited for an interview with the French scientific attaché at his consulate in Chicago. My French was very hesitant, but the interview was all in French. He wanted to gauge not just my skill in French but also my interest in developing it further. I won the scholarship. I was ecstatic. But the scholarship only paid for part of my stay. The French are not as generous as the Americans when it comes to higher studies for foreigners. I believe I would have qualified for a tuition waiver because I hailed from a Third World country, India, but I never asked for it, so never got it.

I had to make money to be able to live in France. It was summertime and it was time to work and earn. I moved to Silicon Valley where I got a very lucrative internship. I fell in love with Silicon Valley immediately. That was in 1997. Twenty-three years later I still live in Silicon Valley, although in the intervening years, I have lived in Atlanta (4 years); Austin (two years); India (a year and a half); Lafayette, Indiana (a year); and Paris (a year). I still like Silicon Valley although its glow has faded over time. Now I really want to move from here. That's what happens with temporal attachments. They fade, they recede over time. But attachment to Jesus? It only glows and grows.

Paris was simply magical. The city of lights, the city of romance, the city of art and fashion, it was everything that I thought it would be and it was much more. Our college campus was located about an hour south of Paris. To get to Paris, one either took the train or drove. We were an eclectic group of students—two Americans, two Mexicans, two Indians, two Poles, two Russians, two Canadians, two Japanese, and one Hungarian. All of us spoke broken French only and that was the only language in common between all of us!

France is considered the eldest daughter of the Church, although the French pay a lot of stress on secularism, or *laicite* as they call it. I discovered though that many of my French friends were strong Catholics. In fact, I fell in love with a very strong Catholic woman, Marie. We were learning the tango and became dance partners. I think both of us were intensely attracted to the other. I asked Marie if she would move to the US with me. She replied, perhaps. The French, like the Indians and the Japanese, never say no. Perhaps for the French can mean anything—yes, no, or just perhaps. I, in my boundless optimism, took it too mean yes. But Marie had many French suitors in the college. Her father was Catholic, and her mother was Protestant, a rare combination in France.

Marie started resisting my overtures. She had told me that she was *sans experience*, which in effect meant that she was a virgin. At 23, I doubt that she had even kissed a man. She was the archetypal Christian girl and perfect marriage material for many. Every time I brought up her strange behavior with me (she waxed at one moment and waned at the other) to our common friends, who were all Catholic, they would respond, oh, that's because her mom is Protestant. People seem to think that all of the French have deserted Christianity and are a people of passion and immorals and whatnot. Such was not my experience in France. The French divide the world in two ways: they themselves are Catholic and Latin, and the Anglo-Saxons (meaning the British, the Americans, and the Germans) are Protestant.

This is not strictly true because half of Germany is Catholic. There are many Catholics in America as well, but when the French are referring to Americans, they are alluding to white Americans only and not to Hispanic Americans. It is this worldview that shapes France. Now the French are not as archetypal Latin as the Italians or the Spanish or the Portuguese. The French have as many northern European characteristics as southern European. For instance, they are not as mercurial or as temperamental as the Italians. But the French will refuse to call themselves anything but Latin. *On est catholiques, on est latins. Ils sont protestants, ils sont anglo-saxons.* This is the refrain one hears all the time in France: We are Catholic, we are Latin. They are Protestants, they are Anglo-Saxons.

The hatred between the French and the British runs deep, and it cuts deep. Strange though then that the Anglican Church is more close to the Catholic Church than any Protestant church. As I have written before, I have visited many Anglican churches in England with Jesus on the cross. In Protestant churches in America, I never saw Jesus on the cross. My knowledge in this respect is limited, as I am still grappling with the complexities of coming to Christ, so if I make any *faux pas*, please forgive me. In any case, my endeavor is to come to Christ, and really not to any specific church.

Marie finally came back to me and said no and said that she was going with another man. I was devastated. I thought she had really loved me. I sought therapy. The therapist was gorgeous. One look at her and I forgot all about Marie. I think the therapist also took a liking to me. I was considered an exotic bird in France. But I had to stay professional with the therapist and she with me. Soon enough she rendered her judgment. Marie had never been in love with me. I was even more devastated. I thought she was the first love of my life, but she turned out to be a fruitless infatuation. I still couldn't get over her. I kept mooning over her. My Indian college mate and my neighbor in the dorm, Soumen, thought that I had gone mad. He told me that there are so many beautiful girls in Paris, yet you are hung up over this not-so-good looking girl in the college, where for every girl there are 10 French suitors. I don't know what had happened to me. I saw purity, Christian purity in Marie and would have happily embraced Christianity if she had accepted me.

The Ecole Polytechnique had only about a thousand students but it was self-contained with its own prayer halls. It had a chapel, and true to French traditions of *laicite*, an Islamic prayer hall and a Jewish prayer room as well. I found myself in a strange culture and because my French was poor, I felt like a five-year old searching for words to express myself. For example, then, I didn't know the French word for knife. So I would find myself hard-pressed to describe to others what I needed when I needed a knife. It was like regaining my infancy and was incredibly fatiguing. By midnight I would be so tired that I would just crash into bed. I needed spiritual solace badly at this time.

I of course was drawn to the chapel and made a number of visits there during the day. It was built in the Jesuit tradition, exactly as the chapels in my schools in India. I was relatively unexposed to Islam and completely unexposed to Judaism, so their prayer rooms held no appeal for me. Jesus it was going to be for me! Praying to Jesus in His own divine presence in the chapel helped me tide over the initial difficult phase in France. Marie's best friend was Sybille. Sybille was attractive but husky, not my type. But she was very friendly and outgoing. I didn't realize that she had a thing for me; I was so busy being besotted by Marie! Sybille invited me home for a formal dinner. Her father was an accomplished lawyer. Her mother and siblings were present. It was all very formal. Just like *Guess Who's Coming for Dinner*. But it didn't feel like that. I was Indian, who are considered several pegs higher than Africans in France. And then I was a student at the Ecole Polytechnique. That broke down all racial barriers in France. I didn't realize then that Sybille was actually showing me to her family for their affirmation of me. She then took me to her room, not for any intimacy but just to hang out.

Sybille was fervently Christian too. She and I started to hang out. On the streets of Paris, we came across a homeless man. Sybille hugged him tightly. She said that you people in America are petrified of the homeless but here in France we have no such fear. I realized that Americans talk a lot about Christianity but put into practice the teachings of Jesus perhaps less than the "secular" French. My discussions with Sybille revolved mostly around Marie. I told her, perhaps Marie would tire of her man and come to me. Sybille admonished me. She said that Marie would be a one-man woman all her life. It was quite funny really. Every other girl I met in France would tell me that how could one stay with one man all one's life. But such is the power of Christian devotion that even in such a freewheeling culture as France's, girls like Marie and Sybille are able to stay loyal to one man all their lives. I still didn't realize that Sybille wanted me to be that one man for her.

They say that it's difficult to integrate into a French group. But the honest truth is I have spent twenty-five years in the US and I have been intimate with a number of women. Not one has ever invited me home to meet her parents and her family as Sybille had done. Once you are accepted in a group in France, you are truly accepted. Sybille invited me to see a play with her friends at a fabled theater in Paris. The play was all about this man who had a statuette of Jesus and fervently believed in it. He went through homelessness and sickness but he never relinquished his faith in the statuette. The play made a deep and abiding impression on me. I wish I could be as devoted to Jesus as the protagonist of the play was.

Later on all of us friends went to have tea in someone's house. The French drink their tea very differently from the British and the Indians. What they call tea is not really tea. It is just boiled water with some herbs thrown in. It comes out looking like green tea. And then the French, so spiteful are they of the British, do not drink tea in a cup and saucer the British way. French tea comes in a bowl, the size of which is somewhere in between a small bowl of soup in a Chinese restaurant and a large bowl of soup. So now you have to hold this bowl of tea in both hands and make sure you don't drop it and then drink this slimy, tasteless broth and pretend that you are drinking some great drink. And unlike the Brits, who must have biscuits or scones or something like that with their tea, the French do not serve any snacks with their tea. So you have nothing to alleviate the horrid taste of the "tea" that you are drinking in France.

It was close to 2 am by now. I of course was the object of curiosity of everyone, this exotic colored species among this all-white French crowd. They didn't know what to make of me really. Many of them had never encountered an Indian before. Here I was an Indian going to their top school. That incited disbelief in them. And then I spoke broken French. How could I have been admitted to their top school with my limited French language skills? To quote Churchill, you could say that I was a riddle wrapped in a mystery inside an enigma. But perhaps there was a key. Yes, there was a key to understand me. I knew the question was coming. And it did. I was tired. I didn't even listen to the question. I stopped the questioner right in his tracks as soon as he raised his hand to ask me the question. I said why not we discuss the matter at a more earthly hour. He was sorely disappointed. So was the rest of the gang. They could have the discussed the issue all night long. The matter at hand of course was the Hindu system of caste. Whenever in the West, a westerner says that he wants to ask me a question, I know exactly what she wants to ask. I ask her not to ask, or if she has asked already, I duck the question.

I moved to downtown Paris for my work-portion of the program, which was at the French cosmetics company, L'Oreal.

Here not a word in English was spoken so my French improved dramatically. There were women everywhere interested in exotic feathers like mine but I was devoted to my work. I still kept in touch with my old friends from the school. Marie, Sybille, and their friends were all fervent Catholics. They had founded a student organization called *Aslive*, which took people afflicted with Down Syndrome for a weekend retreat to the country a couple of times a month. They asked me to join the retreat. I readily obliged. Going to church was an integral part of the program. Sybille was watching me at church. Would I take the biscuit offered by the Catholic priest? Of course I did. That I felt made me even more attractive to her.

Marie showed up at one of the retreats. It was very awkward for me. She took a photo of me with one of the patients. I still have it with me. I met another beautiful girl there called Anne-Sophie. She was becoming a doctor and invited me to dinner at her apartment. She was not the virginal type like Marie, but she was a lovely girl. She seemed quite interested in me. And then at work I met one of the most beautiful women that I have ever met in my life. Her name was Melanie. We went out a couple times for drinks. She remarked that every moment that she had spent with me had been hilarious for her. And she complimented me on my French. She said that I could understand every word of French that she spoke. Yes, that was true. By then, I had worked really hard at my French.

Suddenly the call came. Marie wanted to see me. She invited me to her parents' house. There was nobody there but her. She offered me a frozen steak, which was too bloody for my taste (the French eat their meat very rare when compared to the Americans), but to please her, I forced it down my throat. I still believed that I had a chance with her. She let me talk. I babbled all night long. Before long it was 5 am. I had to go to work that day. She left me at her door. I told her that perhaps in 15–20 years, when we would be in our forties and both divorced, we would meet again and match up. She started crying. She gave me a kiss on the cheek. A real kiss, not just the French *bisous* (which mainly involves the touching of cheeks). She told me that the reason she chose the other man was because he and she had the same education. That was a load of bull. She and I had the same education too, an engineering education. I knew what the real reason was. That her family would not accept the color of my skin.

On the other hand, there was no color prejudice with Sybille, Anne-Sophie, or Melanie. They in fact were attracted to my dark skin color. Sybille's family didn't seem to have a problem with the color of my skin. Marie too appeared to be attracted to my skin color, but I feel that her family objected to it. So be it. Even though L'Oreal offered me a job in France, I had to return to Illinois to wrap up my master's degree. I could of course have returned to France after that, and courted any of the aforementioned girls except of course Marie, but I was not thinking straight. I was not letting Jesus do the thinking for me. I was enticed by the higher job salaries in the States and the booming Internet market there. I had dreams of starting companies and becoming a multi-millionaire. Any of the aforementioned French girls would have made a great wife for me. I never got to start a big company for myself. I am sure that if I had stayed back in France and married any of the girls I had met there, I would have had two or three children by now. I didn't return to France. I stayed back in the US. Twenty-two years later, I am 52, single and issueless. I still want to go back to France and marry a French girl there. But when I had everything as an offering on a plate, I didn't take it. Jesus was being so kind, and I refuted Him. Now I only pray to Jesus, Let Thy Will be done. After my experience in France, and after the huge challenges that I have subsequently gone through with Indian and American girls (save for three Americans: Sonya, Holli, and Shelbey), I would be a fool not to let Jesus take charge of my life. I took charge once, in France, and have suffered immeasurably. Jesus knows how to take care of you. At that time, I was not as close to Jesus, so did not heed His call.

CHAPTER 6

Sonya

In 1998, I returned to Illinois, wrapped up my master's degree and got a job with Dell in Austin. Dell then was an exciting relatively new company. Its stock was surging and it was known for making many of its employees millionaires, or Dellionaires as they liked to call themselves. One career coaching manual described the company as hot, hot, hot. There was no way I wasn't going to join it. The labor market then was as tight as it had ever been. Companies were going on a mad hiring spree. In my case, I never interviewed with the people I was going to work with at Dell. I was just assigned to them by other people in the company who had interviewed me. I didn't even know who my boss was going to be.

Raju was a first cousin of mine who lived in Austin. He was an engineer. He had married a white American woman, Diana. She was strongly Protestant. He had two little children, who he sent to Sunday school. But Diana had adapted to Raju too. She had become an ace Indian cook and entertained his Indian friends regularly. He in turn was thick with her family, who were all strongly Christian. I spent a pleasant weekend at Raju and Diana's. The first week at Dell almost killed me. I became petrified by the pace of work. I called Diana frantically. She invited me to her home the following weekend to calm me down. Because I had not interviewed with any of my colleagues, including my boss, Rick, it was a tough start for me at Dell. One of my peers was Eric. But he behaved as if he was my boss.

He told me that Rick and he had worked together earlier. He gave me assignments to do, for some of which I had to pull in all-nighters, but then he always found glaring errors in my work and complained to Rick. He stored some company T-shirts in the drawer of my desk and then accused me of stealing some. Heavens! If he didn't trust me enough, why did he give the T-shirts to me for safekeeping. One day, in driving rain, he sent me to another branch of the company. I had never driven in such pouring rain before and have never done so since. Visibility was not near zero. It was zero. I could have got myself killed over a routine work matter. Once in a meeting, he started criticizing me. I got up to leave whence he restrained me physically. I started despising Eric.

Eric called me to his home for barbecue. He was all alone. He then confided in me a secret. A slot above Rick was open. Rick was aspiring to fill that slot. If Rick moved there, Eric would get Rick's current position and become my actual boss. I hoped and prayed that such an occurrence would not happen. And then Eric told me that he was a fervent Christian. He asked me about my faith. I said that I was Hindu but that I believed in Christ. Eric invited me to his church. Any church that produced an insensitive person like Eric must not be worth going to. I turned him down, firmly. We were not going to make up, that was for sure.

I used to live in a cheap motel called the Extended Stay America. Every evening, after work, I would hail a cab by dialing from work. She was listening. She was Sonya. She sat right behind me. She told me that she would give me a ride home. So then this became our regular routine. I felt obligated to invite her to my room. Mercifully, she declined. My room was a mess. Sonya worked as a marketing analyst. She hailed from Florence, Alabama. She had a beautiful, refined Southern accent, and not the nasal twang I would get used to later on in life. She was a rich woman. She owned a plantation in Alabama, where her mother lived. Every other weekend she would fly back home.

We started hanging together after work. One day I asked her out for a drink. She invited me to her apartment instead. Her place was beautifully done up. Even in India, I had read a lot about Lincoln and of course read the obligatory *Gone with the Wind*. The minute I brought up Lincoln's name, she scoffed at it. She said that he had extremely long and ugly years. I then realized how much the Southerners hated the Yankees still. Texas was technically not the South during the Civil War even though it sent troops to aid the South. Texans like to think of themselves as Southerners, even though the South still doesn't consider Texas as the South. Still, Southern magazines such as *Southern Living* and *Garden & Gun* are very popular magazines in Texas. In meetings, if there were people visiting us from the Northeast, the whole room would erupt, the Yankees are coming, the Yankees are coming. It was as if the Civil War had never ended.

Sonya was born and raised Christian, although she had become skeptical about God's existence. We became intimate quite quickly. The sin in our hearts overtook us. Sonya me told me that she had become Hindu. She started wearing Hindu symbols. But I knew that she was doing all this only to attract me. I don't understand why people act as if they have converted during courtship, only to revert to type after marriage. That plays havoc with the marriage and can often lead to divorce. Sonya didn't understand. I was perfectly happy marrying a Christian girl. She didn't have to do a fake Hindu makeover for me.

The chemistry between us was great. So was the compatibility. Sonya encouraged me to read a number of classics such as Tolstoy's *War and Peace*, Nathaniel Hawthorne's *The Scarlet Letter*, Dickens' *David Copperfield*, and Iain Piers' *An Instance of the Fingerpost*. Reading these books improved my English greatly. I was also struck by how people in the past had faced the very same situations that we face today. That is why the Holy Bible holds such eternal wisdom. In America, there are an endless number of new-age therapies and ideologies. There is no need for them. The Bible is enough.

My parents were looking for a match for me in India, but because I was entangled with Sonya, I would not return home. One day she tried the classic pregnancy test with him. She was at home and I was at work. She called me to tell me that she was pregnant. I felt really happy. Now we could have the baby, get married and no longer live in sin. But she was playing a game with me to test my commitment to her. I think I passed with flying colors. I didn't go crazy that she had to drop the baby. Thanksgiving came and I asked her to go to New Orleans with me. She said no, she had to return to her mom, although she regretted her action later. She was Southern and I had been led to believe that Southern people were racist. So at Christmas, I told her that I wanted to visit her mother and the rest of her family to make sure that they would accept a person of color like me.

She refused again. She insisted that her family was not racist. A verbal assurance was not enough for me. She said that if she introduced me to her family as her beau, and then if I turned her down, she would lose face in front of her family. I really didn't understand her attitude. Only later when I went to live in Atlanta, I understood that saving face was a big deal for Southern women. Many white Southern women want to get intimate with black men, but only on the sly. They don't want to be seen with black men in public lest they invite the disapprobation of their family and friends. It's all hypocrisy really. But it's a Southern thing. Every culture has its quirks.

Sonya never once mentioned that she wanted to have kids with me. I was desperate for kids. I started moving away from her. It was a long and painful process. We were living in sin and the Devil had seized the both of us. No matter how much we tried, we could not let go of one another. Then Sonya told me that her family was finding a man for her. She begged me to marry her. She was about five years older than me, and while that never bothered me initially, she developed a complex about it and kept talking about it. I myself then could not stop thinking about the age difference. I was 30. She was 35. In India, women as young as 23 were willing to marry me. Sonya said that I would be physically attracted to her for just another 10–15 years, and then I would lose attraction for her and start playing around. I told her no, give me a couple of kids, I'll never play around, I'll just play with them. But then I asked her, what if I strayed, even a tiny little bit. She said that I would become history for her.

I have mainly worked in Corporate America and then I see American TV shows like *The Office*. The workplace seems a great hunting ground to meet the opposite sex. It has always worked for me. Maybe because American women, who would perhaps be hesitant to meet me online, can talk and meet me at work before any amorosity sets in. I am always well-dressed at work, I always try to behave in a gentlemanly manner, the women can see what they are going to get with me. American women have always flocked to me at work like moths to a flame. But there has always been a challenge. I am not white. I am colored. White men rule the roost in America. They in general cannot tolerate it if a white woman passes them over for a colored. Sonya was one of the very few attractive women at Dell. Many white men tried to court her. But they had all figured that she had been taken. By me. Many white men can't understand why a white woman would go with a colored when they are there, right there, the pinnacle of male handsomeness, waiting for them.

I don't understand. Thanks to Jesus, I am not attracted to men. Only to women. Yes, if I see a man, in my mind I can somewhat gauge whether he's attractive or not. But then I see many attractive women out with men I would say are not attractive. I have foregone figuring out which man is attractive or not. It doesn't bother me. I couldn't care less. I am not attracted to them. As far as I am concerned, any woman can go out with any man. Any Indian woman can go out with any man, including black men. I am not the guardian of the virtuosity of women. Initially when I was with Sonya, I used to say that I was attracted to her because she was white and therefore I was racist in an inverse sort of way. She responded, you can be attracted to any color. That doesn't make you a racist or not. Her words really comforted me.

In any case, my dalliance with Sonya was ruffling a lot of white feathers at Dell and causing a lot of jealousy. My admin, Deborah, who was a very attractive New Yorker, and who had made her intentions about me clear to me from day one, suddenly arrived at my apartment and barged straight into my bedroom. I knew what she wanted, but I was not going to give it to her. I knew I was living in sin with Sonya, but at least I was loyal to her. As long as I was with her, I would not go anywhere else. Sonya and I kept our relationship completely professional at work. We would not even indulge in any form of PDA at work. But still people got to know that we were together. Just recently I was seeing an episode of *Saturday Night Live* and the comedian said that during the time of slavery and Jim Crow, when a white woman snuck away to have sex with a black man and was caught in the act, she would say that it was nonconsensual. Guess who got guillotined then? It was the black man. That has been the history of America. That is the reality of America even today. That is going to be the future of America for a long time to come.

I was disciplined by my boss. Deborah said that they are going after you because you are a minority. Sonya brushed that off, but said that she would take up my case with her boss, the vice president of the division, with whom she had an excellent rapport. Those days I was much more immature and rigid than I am now. Today, if such a thing were to happen to me, I would have happily told Sonya to go right ahead and try to save me. It makes sense to try any and everything while swimming with sharks. But those days I was much too proud and haughty. I told Sonya that I was man enough to deal with the situation myself. I restrained her from approaching her boss. As expected I got the axe. It was a stunning blow, especially since I used to work very hard.

Over the summer, we had a couple of MBA interns visiting from Cornell. One of them was a woman. She figured out that Sonya and I were together and counseled me to marry her. But at that time Sonya and I were in the very beginning stages of our relationship. Neither of us wanted to lunge headlong into marriage. Sonya was divorced. I wanted a significant amount of courtship to

happen and some kinks in my mind ironed out before I committed myself. In any case, the MBA intern, Sally, became a friend of
mine. One day she said that she and a woman friend of hers were
driving down to a very famous barbecue joint in Austin called *The
Salt Lick BBQ* and asked me if I would care to join them. In 1998
Austin was not a large city. One could cover one end of town to the
other in about 45 minutes. The barbecue joint was located deep in
the woods. Suddenly a golden dome appeared. I recognized it for
what it was, a Hindu temple. Sally's friend asked what the building
was. I was sitting in the back seat and slunk into my seat. Fortunately Sally answered the question correctly. I was so glad that
they didn't ask me anything. The moment passed. We drove by the
temple. It receded quickly into the background. Those days I was
ashamed of my Hinduness and liked to hide it. Little did I realize
how big a role the temple would play in my life in the ensuing
years.

At the barbecue itself, I was busy chomping away on beef
when a young couple from North Carolina asked if I was Hindu.
I said yes. They asked isn't eating beef forbidden in Hinduism. I
responded that Hinduism is a very laid-back, *laissez-faire* religion,
which doesn't prohibit you from doing anything. Yes, the cow is
considered sacred in Hinduism, but just because you start eating
beef, that does not stop you from being a Hindu. Many Hindus in
the West, and even in India itself, eat beef.

Since things with Sonya were not working out, and I had
been scalded by my experience at Dell, I wanted to move to Silicon
Valley where I knew that many of my brethren, my fellow Indians,
worked, and where I thought that I would naturally face less racism than I had faced in an almost all-white culture such as Dell's. I
asked Sonya if she would move to California. Like many Southerners, she disliked California. She didn't care for the density of the
population nor for the notorious traffic. It was a difficult time for
me. My mom was visiting from India. I made her meet Sonya a few
times. The three of us went out for dinner a couple of times. My
mother and Sonya got along like a house on fire. I didn't introduce
Sonya to my mother as my girlfriend. I told her that she was only

a colleague. I was too embarrassed to tell my mother that I was living in sin with someone, especially with a woman who was not Indian. I thought my mother would wise up to the fact that Sonya and I were dating but she feigned ignorance. Later on she told that she would have given me the go-ahead to marry Sonya if I had told her that I was seeing her.

Since childhood, my mother and I have had a complicated relationship. How could she not see that Sonya and I were together? My American friend, Robert, used to come have dinner with my mother and me regularly, but I never introduced my mother to any other woman but Sonya. Sonya baked a delicious cake for my mom. How could my mother not see that something was going on between us? Perhaps she didn't want to get involved. Making a decision for her Indian son to marry a white woman, and that too one significantly older than him, might have proven too big a decision for her to make alone. Perhaps she needed my dad's guidance. But he was in India and had never met Sonya. And Sonya was fast moving towards getting remarried to someone else. There was no time to insert my dad in the process. By that time Sonya had figured out that I would not say yes to her. Even by chance if I had proposed to her, contingent on my parents' approval, she would not have waited. Indian parents shy away from their kids marrying Americans not just because of the difference in religion and culture. Indian people think that westerners get divorced too easily. For most Indians, marriage is for life and divorce is a lifelong stigma. Perhaps that's why my mom kept her cards close to her chest. She did not want to see me getting divorced. And it could have happened. Sonya was so wedded to her plantation in Florence, Alabama, that she would have forced me to move there. I would have been miserable there. First my work would have made me fly to other cities because there is literally nothing in Florence. Secondly, even I had become a writer as I have become now, I would never have seen people of my own kind, Indians, in Florence, and would have wanted to live somewhere else. I am sure where we settled down would have become a bone of significant contention between Sonya and me.

This was the one instance where the LORD's unseen but magical hands helped me. It was the one time when I let His Will be done. Two decades later, I still miss Sonya. I am single and will gladly have her back if she would like to come back to me. I still call her at times. I don't even know if she's married or single. She always slams her phone. She says that I rejected her. That I used her for sex, for her white skin. That's simply preposterous. Then she too used me for sex, for my brown skin. In a weak moment she let on that she didn't want to be with a former lover. So be it. I would still like to talk to her and have a purely platonic relationship with her. But she doesn't seem to have forgiven me. She doesn't pray to Jesus. If she would let Jesus into her heart, she would realize that I had been fully committed to her. I passed her pregnancy test. She was the one who wouldn't let me meet her family. That may have been for good reason from her side, but I didn't understand Southern culture then. So all's well that ends well. I feel nothing but the best for her. She's the only woman I have really known all my 52 years. We thought we were made for each other, but the LORD, the sweet LORD Jesus, in all his omniscience didn't let us stay together.

My mother would cook a simple meal every night and we would visit the Hindu temple, the one I had shied away from, and after religious service, sit next to the fountain at the back of the temple and have our meal in the moonlight. It was really beautiful. I should never have left Austin. Now that Sonya and I had parted ways, she dropped the façade of her being Hindu and declared that she had been raised Christian. One day she was an atheist, the next a Hindu, then a Christian. It all seemed too convenient to me. There was no meeting of the spiritual minds with her.

CHAPTER 7

Trying to Become
a Devout Hindu

After the traumatizing experience at Dell in Austin, I just had to succeed in Silicon Valley. My brother urged me to quit marketing and go back to engineering, which was more in line with my education. But I loved marketing and hated engineering. My brother counseled that in Corporate America, to survive and even succeed, one's job is 80% working and 20% sucking up to the boss. My father too counseled that I needed to get along with my boss. I had not told them about Sonya and about what had happened with the white boys at Dell. I just sucked in whatever they said.

It takes a day to get out of Texas. I put my meager belongings in my Honda sedan and started driving toward California. I had had a severe bout of pneumonial bronchitis just before I left but I knew that Jesus would give me the strength to overcome that and leave for California. I was so taken by the Hindu temple in Austin and the preachers there that I decided that I would attend the branch of the temple in San Jose, California when I reached there. I thought that I would not get into any trouble at my job in California if I kept attending my Hindu religious service. The drive in Texas was very isolated. For miles no car or truck would cross you. I opened the moonroof of my car. It was as if the heavens with all their twinkling stars would fall inside. I looked outside my side window and was completely bewitched. It seemed that God and Jesus and my Hindu god had created this blessed scenery for me. I had never ever felt so close to Nature. I had to be careful though lest I stray into the opposite lane, this stretch of highway all being two-lane.

I decided to make my way to the Grand Canyon. It really was magnificent, one of the natural wonders of the world. What a chasm God had wrought. I thought of going down to the Colorado River and do whitewater rafting there. My friend had done it and had raved about it to me. But one-quarter of the way down, better sense prevailed and I made my way back up. Nature is so beautiful. It's God's way of reminding us that He exists and that He has power over us, no matter how boundlessly optimistic man becomes about his supposed strength. I reached San Jose after four days on the road and immediately called Sonya from my office. She was delighted to hear from me. The next few months would bring tears of misery to me. Austin had two highways. Silicon Valley had between 15–20. I used to keep getting lost, especially at night. GPS was not popular then. I used to cry out loud for Sonya. Now I knew how much I missed her and how much I loved her. She had gotten married immediately after I quit Austin. I wanted to go back to her. If she would have me, I would have gone back to Austin straightway. But her door was closed forever it seemed now. Meanwhile, I was stranded in California!

I walked straightway into a political trap at my new job. My boss had hired me but a couple of other senior managers resented my presence. They thought that my job lay in their bailiwick. I quickly called the branch of the Hindu temple. The man on the other line urged me to attend as soon as possible. The service would be held at the house of a Croatian, his Croatian wife, and their two beautiful young daughters. The service was beatific with a TV sermon from a guru. It gave me the courage to take the high road at work and work with the politics. That saved my job. But the Croatian was fervent. On my very first visit he urged me to buy cassettes of the guru's sermons. I told him that I didn't have a cassette player. He said then go buy it. I was not buying anything until I settled into an apartment. I was staying at an Extended Stay America motel an hour and a half from work. I had much to do in California before I bought a cassette player to listen to the guru's sermons. I felt that the Croat just wanted to make money from selling the cassettes to me. Yet I kept going to the religious service. I knew nobody in California except my brother and sister who lived more than an hour away from me and were busy raising their young kids. So the service was a welcome diversion from work. It conformed to my schedule and lasted only an hour.

After the service, I would play basketball or soccer with the Croat's girls. I could see that he was not entirely comfortable with me playing with his daughters. What did he think, that I was some kind of pedophiliac who would harm his girls? I mean, I was a part of his religious order. He could have got my credentials veri- fied from the temple in Austin. As I spent more and more time in the religious service, I realized that there was an undercurrent of suspicion everywhere. Another woman, Donna, a Catholic turned Hindu, lived in the Croat's house along with her mother. She was a nice, docile woman, but she said that Catholicism instilled in one a lot of guilt and that's why she had left the fold. My exposure to Catholicism had not been one of guilt, instead one of love and forgiveness, so I kept quiet.

The girls I played with started behaving weirdly with me. We met at a large Hindu temple in San Jose where they acted as if they didn't know me. Then we met at Costco. Again they blithely ignored me even though they had seen me. I felt insulted. I was only trying to be nice to them by playing with them. If they didn't want to play with me, they could have stopped doing so. But my word, why were they insulting me so now? There seemed some- thing amiss with the religious service. I suddenly learned that my beloved dad had passed away in India. I rushed home for his funeral. He had visited me in San Jose just before he died. He saw an American flag in my house. He said that he liked the flag and instructed me that I must retain it. That was his last piece of advice to me. I still have the flag in my house.

There was tremendous pressure for me to get married in India. My relatives fixed me up with a traditional Hindu woman. I brought my wife with me to San Jose. She did her normal Hindu prayers in the morning and didn't care about going to any temple or religious service. But I took her to the Croat's house. The Croat's wife asked us when we were going to have babies. It was a strange question because the guru emphasized celibacy. I knew something was wrong somewhere.

One day I went alone for the service (my wife having begged leave), and found that the Croat's house was closed. I didn't know what had happened. I learned later that he had had a falling out with the guru. I believe it was something to do with his daughters. Donna and her mother left his house and rented a modest apartment. Now the service would be held there. The Croat was no longer welcome in Donna's house. There had been a real falling out within the group. My wife and I proved simply incompatible. The next two and a half years got spent in retrieving my marriage. I stopped going to the religious service and sought marital counseling instead. The counselor said that your marriage is an absolute no-go. I still thought I could save it.

On a business visit to Rome, I visited St. Peter's Basilica in Vatican City. I had become used to confessing in my Catholic schools and so stood in line at St. Peter's to confess. A jerk came up to me and said that because I was not Christian, I could not confess. How did he know that I was not Christian? Because I looked Indian? But many Indians were Christian. I simply ignored him and complained about him to the priest in the confessional chamber. The priest told me to just forget about the jerk. The priest was a kindly man who spoke English with a decided Italian accent. I explained my marital situation to him. He responded that I had made a commitment, so I had to keep it. I told him that there was no chemistry in our marriage. He got it, finally. He said that so you two are living like father and daughter, brother and sister. I said exactly. He said then leave her but be generous with her. I took his advice to heart. I was simply amazed. I had been led to believe that the Catholic church was dead-set against divorce, but here was a priest in St. Peter's Basilica itself who had heard me out and given me the go-ahead.

I took a tour of the Vatican. Ahead of me was an old Irish couple. The woman kept referring to me as love. Love this, love that. She seemed incredibly warm. I just love the Irish. If people in Ireland are as warm and friendly and dare I say, as lovely, as the Irishwoman, I would happily move to Ireland. Then I went on the roof of the Vatican and saw the statues of Jesus and the Twelve Apostles. It was a magnificent sight. I spent hours on the roof and found it hard to tear myself away. I had come to Jesus and he had resolved a problem of mine that was proving intractable and eating my insides. I returned home to California with the firm resolve of filing for divorce, which I did, and as per the priest's advice, gave my wife every penny that was due her. I walked away from the divorce without any guilt, thanks to Jesus. Donna was simply wrong when she claimed that Catholicism bred guilt in you.

Now the service was being held at Donna's house. I was going through a messy divorce. So I attended the service regularly just to keep my head afloat in life. The preacher assigned to our center from the headquarters in Austin was a tyrant. She was a Gujarati Indian woman born and raised in Fiji. (Gujarat is a state in India.) She didn't take kindly to me. She got along in the main only with Gujarati folks. Donna rented a bigger house. I was asked to help her move. There were two much younger, sturdier boys than me who had promised to help Donna move, but they did nothing as I went about the move. The whole load fell on me. The preacher liked the other boys and kept gabbing with them. At the end of the move, she ordered pizza for all of us, but I begged off. The other two boys, who had done virtually nothing, happily chomped on the pizza. I was disgusted. How could the preacher not see who was working and who was not and even worse, condone the people who had been remiss?

The preacher assigned us to clean Donna's house every Saturday at 7 am. That was simply unsustainable. Saturday morning, after a hard week's work, was sleep-in time. Still I made it to Donna's house at 7. I was assigned the job of hosing down the house. I was always assigned the toughest jobs by the preacher. By mistake I hosed down the front door, not realizing that the wooden door at the back of the grill, which was shut, was open. Water filled the entrance of the house. The preacher became apoplectic. She screamed, "How dare you flood Donna's house?" But it was an honest mistake. I was cleaning the whole house and didn't realize that a door was open because it was hidden by a grill. I started hating the preacher but at the same time became fearful of her. Her guru's message was one of love. He once gave a sermon on Jesus and described how loving, how kind, how gentle Jesus was. The preacher was the guru's premier acolyte. He had raised her as his daughter because he too had lived in Fiji. But she just bred fear and resentment, not just in me but in other disciples as well. We complained to the guru about her, but he didn't do anything. He said just see the good in her.

I was already a life member of the Hindu temple, which cost a healthy thousand dollars. In Hindu scriptures, the tithe is 10% of one's earnings, and the guru and his preachers would counsel us regularly to give that amount. They would say that the 10% tithe in Catholicism came from Hinduism to prove that Hinduism was the precursor of all religions. I was going through an expensive divorce but I made sure that I tried to give as much as I could. I used to unfailingly donate $60 every week to the religious service in Donna's house. She noticed my generosity and asked me to pay for her new computer, which I did. She also asked me to write something in English for her, which I did, but then said that she would ask two Americans instead because they were native speakers of English and I was not. I felt really insulted because my first language was English, and she knew it.

The preacher's insults labored on. The guru's sermons would invariably be in Hindi. Many Indians do not speak Hindi, so I would be asked to translate the sermon into English. It was a tough task translating a 45-minute sermon into English but I took to the task with uncommon zeal. People really liked my translation and said that I did a word for word job. Instead of applauding me, the preacher switched my job. Now I was supposed to vacuum the whole house before the service started. The task of translation was assigned to someone else. My talents were being wasted and everybody knew it. The preacher was not even divine; the guru used to say that all the preachers were just like devotees, simply seekers on the path towards enlightenment. I don't know what I had done to tick off this Hitleresque preacher. She certainly wasn't endearing me to her religious order.

During my divorce, which took two years from 2004–06, I used to visit the Austin temple about once a year. It was spread over 200 acres and was really beautiful. I noticed this Indian woman making eyes at me. But I didn't like to mix spirituality with temporal pleasures. I had a discussion with a young woman at a Baptist church in Atlanta many years later. She claimed what was the harm if two like-minded people met at church. I was still unconvinced. If I wanted a woman, I could find her elsewhere from a temple or a church. At the Austin temple, I bumped across an American woman who I was really attracted to and who seemed interested in me, but I resisted the urge to approach her.

The Austin temple held an annual fete with Indian food and treats and Indian cultural songs and dances. It used to be a massive hit in the local community and also the primary fundraiser for the temple. The temple had many preachers and staff in residence. Many of the preachers would fly all over the country, and sometimes all over the world. All of this required money. The person who I was most enamored of in the temple was an American guy who led the prayers. He seemed so serene and calm and devoted. I would have loved to be like him. I worshipped the ground he walked on. For the fete, I was assigned to work the lemonade stand. It was summertime. People were thirsty. The job was busy and tough. Most of Austin's considerable Indian community would show up at the fete. Many Americans too would come. Most came for the food and the cultural events. Some were curious about Hinduism. But at that moment I was not peddling Hinduism. I was peddling lemonade, and that too for the first time in my life. I wanted to do a good job to earn lots of money for the temple. No, not, a good job. A great job. I thought that the very existence of the temple depended upon how the lemonade stand performed. Just jokin', but it was somewhat akin to that. That's what we had been told by the temple's staff.

In any case, four people manned the stand. The man who led the prayers and who I idolized as the ideal devotee showed up and talked to an old associate of his who was also working the stand. He gave him the money box and told him not to let it out of his sight. I was completely stunned! So I had spent a thousand dollars flying from San Jose to Austin and the only thing on my mind was to pinch a few dollars from the lemonade money box, money that I was helping generate in the first instance. I was well and truly disgusted. I wanted to quit there and then, but a friend refrained me from doing so. All these people appeared to put on a big show of religion and spirituality and all that jazz, while all they were interested in was pure lucre to pay their way through life. From 10 am when the stand opened to 6 pm when it closed, I was on my feet constantly screaming *Nimbu Paani, Nimbu Paani* (Lemonade, lemonade for a dollar). I think we made a healthy two grand that day, but I lost my voice. As also my feet.

Apart from my friend, who was just a devotee like myself, it seemed that one could not confide in anybody at the temple. I should have been able to talk to my preacher but she, as I have related to you ad nauseam, was a tyrant. The other preachers all seemed to live in la-la land. They didn't seem to have a care in the world that many preachers and staff of the temple were misbehaving with devotees. They seemed to leave all this to the karma of the devotees. I too thought that the stringent tests that my preacher was putting me through were all to the good. That somehow if I tried hard enough and came out with flying colors, I would reach God. But the preacher herself, by the guru's own admission, was not God-realized. How could someone who was not God-realized make me realize God? I didn't get any answers to my questions, so I stopped visiting the temple, although I must confess that the Texan blue bonnets and other red flowers that I saw in the lawns of the temple made for one of the prettiest sights I have ever seen. It was a sea of all shades of blue intermingled with a dark piercing shade of maroon.

I was lost spiritually. I had been cast aside. Another preacher was visiting from India. The guru was based in India and he let his preachers roam the world as they wished. Many of the preachers clashed with one another. For instance, this new preacher from India was not welcome at the Austin temple. He had superb educational qualifications, which he touted greatly in his bio. He had been to two of the best colleges in India, the Indian Institute of Technology, Delhi and the Indian Institute of Management, Calcutta. Many Indians who came to his sermons came because they were impressed by his educational qualifications and to explore why a supremely qualified man like him had renounced the world.

North Indians are typically fairer-skinned that South Indians. Even though I am a North Indian, I am a couple of shades darker than the average North Indian. In India, many people see a dark-skinned person and automatically assume that he's a South Indian. I have been asked many times by Indians if I was South Indian. It is actually quite impolitic to do so. I was once stunned when a professor at Stanford too, who I was meeting for the first time, blurted out, Oh, you must be South Indian. Associating a region with a skin tone does not seem to me to be politically correct. I was sitting next to the preacher visiting from India. He said, Oh, you must be South Indian. I responded, no, I am from Delhi, from the north. The preacher was from the north and just about two shades lighter than me. I was taken aback. I thought that this sophisticated preacher would at least know better than to make a politically incorrect rush to judgment. But I guess educational degrees don't necessarily make one an international sophisticate.

The preacher had big plans to build a Sanskrit university in India. It would cost in the millions of dollars. The primary purpose of his trip to the US was to raise money for his pet project. I was taken in by his sermons and used to cry regularly in them. These were pure tears of devotion. The preacher noticed how attached I had become to him. He asked me to donate $10,000 for his cause.

At that time I was unemployed. My mother was visiting me in the US and attended the preacher's sermons with me. She too admired the preacher and counseled me to pay the money to him in installments. I sent him the first sum of $2000 but nothing after that.

The preacher arranged a retreat for his devotees in Dallas. I flew there from San Jose. The schedule was arduous. We would be up at 4 am. I met a Hindu man from Bangladesh who was married to a Japanese woman. He apprised me about the atrocities being committed by the Muslims of Bangladesh against the Hindus of Bangladesh. He was a scientist. He had a brought along a son of his who was in high school. The preacher had assigned us a topic to write an essay on. I spent a couple hours helping the scientist's son write his essay and then wrote my own. The winner of the essay competition was going to be announced, but at the last minute the preacher said no, the results won't be announced. I felt disappointed because I felt that I was the winner. Perhaps the preacher felt that my background was far superior to the others, so it would not be fair to them if he declared me the winner.

I was nearing forty, yet dressed in my Indian clothes, I looked much younger. People came up to me asking if I was in college. My looks were all thanks to the grace of God. The Indian woman who I had met in Austin was present here again in Dallas, and was once again making eyes at me. I averted my eyes from her. I had come on a spiritual retreat, not to mate. I was so impressed by the preacher that I thought about becoming a Hindu preacher myself and take *sanyas* (renunciation from the world). But then I realized that I was just craving all the attention that the preacher was getting from his devotees. I wanted to be up on the stage too and lecture the world. That was no reason to become a preacher. And *sanyas* entailed becoming celibate, which I was not willing to become.

So I dropped the idea of becoming a preacher. Back in San Jose, I met the Bangladeshi scientist. He had a US government grant to do research on solar cells. He wanted to hire someone to help him with the strategy of going to market. He was a one-man band with no product or staff. He offered me a lowly salary. I thought what? We are fellow devotees. I just spent hours training your son. Yet, you are low-balling me so badly. Donna told me that Peter, one of the principal devotees of the *ashram* (temple) in Austin, ran a multi-million dollar marketing firm. I was a man in marketing. I expectantly sent him my resume. He did not even care to respond. After that I decided never to seek help from my fellow devotees again. They showed one face during the religious service, a face of piety and generosity, but when they stepped into the temporal world, they revealed their mean selves.

My religious group was miffed at what they felt was the mis-representation of Hinduism in Californian textbooks. They want-ed me to become a part of their endeavor to change the textbooks. But I felt that we were entering on political terrain now and wanted no part of this enterprise. I was anyway having a tough time find-ing a job. Then I donated enough money to my religious group. I just didn't have more to give, especially to a cause I didn't believe in. I came to God to seek peace and serenity. I didn't want to get worked up over this affront by someone or that affront by someone else. I just felt that we Hindus were in a foreign land, and if we comported ourselves well, local people would get to see who we were and correct their misperceptions about us accordingly. The rest of my group didn't agree with my passive approach. I felt that I was becoming an outcaste in my group. I was moving away. I was moving away to something more spiritual, more heavenly, more godly. In any case, the panoply of gods and goddesses in Hinduism confused me utterly. It was just a matter of time before I found my true beloved.

CHAPTER 8

Becoming a US Citizen

My American green card had come in 2002 itself. In five years I would be eligible for my US citizenship. I had to visit Europe regularly for business and would travel on my Indian passport. For each trip I would need a new visa. It was proving to be an onerous task. I missed a couple meetings in Europe because I didn't get my visa on time. Missing important meetings was not helping my career in any way.

Yet, I didn't want to give up my Indian citizenship. I loved living in the States but I was wed to my mother country, India. My loyalty, all my fidelity lay with India. I felt that I was prospering by working in the US, but I was also making the US prosper through my professional contributions. So I put acquiring the US citizenship out of my mind until an Indian friend, Raghav, counseled me otherwise.

The time was around 2005. The US had just invaded Iraq. I felt it in my bones that a terrorist attack would erupt in the US. So did Raghav. He felt that if a major attack like 9/11 were to happen again in the US, the country might stop awarding its citizenship to people like me from the Third World. He insisted that I apply for the US citizenship. Then he said, forget about loyalty and fidelity, you travel overseas so often, just regard the US citizenship as a travel document. A US passport would make it much easier to travel around the world than an Indian passport.

Yet this seemed like making a choice of convenience. The burden played on my mind. I prayed to God and to Jesus and to my Hindu gods. One of the issues that bothered me was that I was moving away from a Hindu-majority country like India to a Christian-majority country like the US. Was I going to become a turncoat to my faith? In the unlikely event if the US went to war with India, which country would I support? These were big questions. I prayed and prayed for light and guidance. Then it came to me. I could remain Hindu in America. America allowed all faiths to proper. As far as war between the US and India was concerned, the two countries were strategic partners. They would never go to war, at least in my lifetime.

The possibility of a terror attack weighed heavily on my mind. I didn't want the US shutting its doors on me. I had been in the country most of my adult life. I knew no other country as well as I knew the US. I liked no other country as much as I liked the US. So I went with my gut and applied for the US citizenship. It was a simple application process really, which I accomplished without hiring a lawyer. The time came for my swearing-in. I had read the US Constitution. It required me to bear arms on behalf of my new country. The Iraq war by 2006 was going very badly. In any case, I, like so many others, felt that it had been wrong to invade the country. My father had spent three years working in Iraq. I was attached to the country and its people. I was repelled by the US invasion to invade Iraq in 2003.

Would I then bear arms for the US if it went to war in an unjust cause like say what happened in Iraq? Or would I prove to be a conscientious objector? I thought I would fight for the country in all just wars. But my father had been a professional soldier in the Indian army. I was a classic military brat. Military brats don't ask their fathers when they are fighting wars if they are fighting just or unjust wars.

Whichever war India sent my father to fight, he fought. He fought two wars against Pakistan. He fought in the Belgian Congo in 1962 as part of the UN blue beret peacekeeping mission. He quelled numerous insurgencies in India. The insurgencies could be seen as those instigated by people fighting in a just cause. Quelling them just to maintain the sovereignty and territory of India could be seen as an unjust reprisal. Yet my father didn't question which fight he fought was just and which fight he fought was unjust. He had taken an oath to fight for India no matter what and that is what he did all his life.

I too decided not to take the oath to bear arms for the US half-heartedly. If the US went to war, and required me to fight, I would fight for the country. Even if the US went to war against India, an unlikely event as I have delineated before, I would fight for the US wholeheartedly. India didn't allow dual citizenship. I was shedding my Indianness, fully, to become a full American. It was one of the proudest and happiest days in my life when I raised my hand to swear allegiance to the Constitution of the United States and when I took the oath to uphold it no matter what. I was now an American citizen. I wanted to assimilate more and more into America. I wanted to adapt to American ways. I didn't realize it then but by acquiring American citizenship, God was taking me to Christ slowly but surely. May God bless all of America! And the whole world!! And may peace prevail on the entire earth!!!

CHAPTER 9

Atlanta and Falling Out of the Hindu Fold

By the grace of God, I finally got a senior job with a famous company called PE in Atlanta in 2008. I really didn't want to move to Atlanta. The previous year another company had invited me for an interview to Atlanta. I made my way to downtown Atlanta then. It was a scary place even during the day. There were cops riding bikes everywhere and keeping a strict vigil. I went and bought an ice cream and sat outside to eat it, but kept watching my back. I didn't want to move to such a fearful place. But by 1998, I had had enough. I had been out of a job two and a half years. My funds were running low. The Great Recession had struck. My sector, green energy, had practically collapsed. I was just so fortunate to get what looked like a great job.

But great it was not. Firstly, the move from Silicon Valley to Atlanta was traumatic. The Deep South has a lot of things going for it but racism is not one of them. Silicon Valley has racism too but it is more subtle, more subliminal than that in the Deep South. In the Deep South they throw racism into your face and then gloat over it. My job had been coveted by many people internal to the company. They hated it when management brought in an outsider like me to fill the job. That I was colored and bossing over them irritated them even more. The first thing I did upon reaching Atlanta was what I had done when I arrived in Silicon Valley from Austin eight years ago. I reached out to find my Hindu religious service.

The service in Atlanta was led by a preacher based in Toronto. She did not get along with the lead preacher in the Austin temple and thus ran her own show. The problem was that each week only two or three people attended her religious service. There was the president of the local chapter, who was a single woman who worked as a researcher at the Center for Disease Control and Prevention in Atlanta. She worked her 9 to 5 job and then dedicated herself fully to whatever the preacher asked her to do. Then there was a self-employed engineer who had worked as a contractor for PE. He was all praises for the company and his experience there. The engineer was the secretary of the organization.

The Hindu order promoted celibacy for its devotees. That was a tall order. They wanted devotees to remain single and dedicate all their time and money to the propagation of their version of Hinduism. Hinduism is a very laid-back *laissez-faire* religion, but these guys were ultra-orthodox and super-strict. And then my friend in the Austin temple, who had urged me not to quit the lemonade stand, told me a dirty little secret. He actually lived in Silicon Valley with his wife. He was an engineer making good money. The preacher who had visited Silicon Valley from India to build his Sanskrit university in India had asked this friend of mine to donate all his salary to his cause. My friend was stunned. He didn't plan to have children because of his devotion to the order, which greatly upset his wife, but how was he going to support himself and his wife if he gave away all his salary? Such unreasonable remands percolated the entire Hindu order. The preachers made it out that if you gave money to them, God would give you manifold in return. What hogwash!

The secretary of the Atlanta order was a married man. But his wife hated the order. She never came to the service. It was obvious that the two didn't have proper conjugal relations. It seemed that she wanted them, but the secretary didn't. This was against all

Hindu principles. Hinduism doesn't promote celibacy for married couples. If the service was ever held at the secretary's house, his wife was practically hostile to everyone attending. She didn't even get along with the preacher. In fact, she considered the influence that the preacher had on her "delinquent" husband as the source of all her problems. As a traditional Hindu wife, she bore her misery though. Divorce is taboo in Hinduism. My friend in Silicon Valley told me that his in-laws in India had urged him not to become celibate, but he had told them not to interfere in his personal matters. So there the matter rested. Both the wives, of the secretary in Atlanta and of my friend in Silicon Valley, were trapped in unhappy marriages. Both the wives wanted children but their "devotee" husbands would not let them have them. It was ironic though that head guru of the whole organization was happily married and had five children, three daughters and two sons, and numerous grandchildren. But if you ever brought that up, you were told that theirs was a "divine" family. We were instructed to do not as what the head guru did, but to do as he told. This was all becoming quite hypocritical to me.

I was single and very keen to get married and settle down and have children. Sometimes I wondered what I was getting into when I noticed what these guys in my religious order were up to. The job in Atlanta was proving difficult. My human resources manager wanted to sleep with me. After my office romance with Sonya in Austin had gone awry for me, I had decided to forsake all office romances. The HR manager was attractive. She got mad when I spurned her. Hell hath no fury as a woman scorned! Then a black manager wanted to date me. And my own 60-year old secretary, a married woman, wanted to have sex with me. I sure was getting really popular! I had come to PE to do some real work, and all I was ending up being was some sort of Indian gigolo. The women who I had rejected made my life miserable. I knew that it was merely a matter of time till I was ejected from the company.

It was all funny really. If you satisfy the sexual urges of white women in America at work, then the white boys get miffed at you for consorting with one of their kind. And if you spurn the women, then they get mad. It was a no-win situation for me. But I had too many morals, too many Christian morals imbibed from school, too many Hindu morals imbibed from life, to start playing around, especially at work.

When I look back at my life, I sometimes wonder where I would have been if I had dated the HR manager. She was a very senior person in the company, having spent over 20 years there. She knew all the top executives in the company. In a huge organization like PE, you were toast if you didn't have a godfather or a fairy godmother. And with the HR manager, I had a brilliant opportunity to cultivate my fairy godmother. I would have gone far at PE if I had coupled with her. Perhaps I might even have been a senior vice-president there today drawing over half a million dollars in salary.

But I gave it all up. All the while the secretary of my religious order kept telling me what a great company PE was. I wanted to tell him to shut up. My experience was entirely different. I was going through hell. And I was going through hell in my personal life as well. I had been denied an apartment because of the color of my skin. The Deep South was a real culture shock from Silicon Valley. But I didn't complain much about my situation at the religious service. I just did what I had always done. I went to the service, kept mum, listened to the sermon and did the chanting, and left quietly. It was the president of the club, the CDC researcher, who publicly kept empathizing with me how different and tough Atlanta must be for me. The secretary made it out as if I was the one doing the bitching. He didn't like me one bit for it.

The preacher arrived from Toronto. I enrolled in her chapter, her own private religious club. That was an additional $500. I was single and flush with money. I kept plying the club with money. But wait a minute. I stopped in my tracks! The preacher wanted to build a million-dollar temple for herself in Atlanta. We were barely three or four people who attended her service regularly. We were all people with a fixed income. Where would we get the money from? And didn't Atlanta already have so many Hindu temples? I expressed my skepticism over the preacher's temple. That didn't go down well with the rest of the group.

Donna, the American woman who ran the religious service in Silicon Valley, used to run it very efficiently. Each service was precisely an hour and ten minutes. There was a video sermon by the head guru, who told us that we should not look hither and thither at other devotees to see if they had developed tears of devotion or not. There was no socializing before or after the service, except on festive days, when food would typically be served after the service. Tears of devotion used to run down my cheeks because I used to concentrate so hard on the sermon and the chantings that followed it afterwards. That was because I didn't expend my energy by talking to the other devotees.

In Atlanta, the situation was very different. The CDC researcher ran the program very loosely. Each service was meant to last an hour and a half but it would drag on for between three and four hours. It would also always start half-an-hour late. Then there would be endless chantings, which were led by kids of the devotees as well. Then there would be a break before the video sermon, during which people would socialize and chit-chat. Nobody seemed really interested in the video sermon because there was always food to follow. I never indulged in idle chit-chat with anyone. I would cry constantly during the sermon. One day the president came up to me and asked me how did I cry so easily, while it was impossible for her to shed tears of devotion. I didn't tell her anything but thought, first and in the main, you are flouting the guru's diktat, which is not to look hither and thither during the service. Second, I wanted her to get how she would shed tears of devotion when she expended all her energy chit-chatting and gossiping with other devotees and not concentrating on the service. I felt the urge to speak out but I refrained. Each devotee there felt that they were the master-guru, the ideal disciple. I politely brushed her question away.

I would not partake in any of the temple-planning activities. This was not taken kindly by the Atlanta preacher, the president of the club or the secretary. But I just couldn't do so. I had been without a job for two and a half years. I just didn't have the money to blow up on a million-dollar temple. And I had a tough job at

PE. I couldn't spend endless hours trying to raise money for the temple or planning its construction. One day I came to the service and met a frosty reception. The secretary, who really admired PE, made me look like a fool for facing difficulty at my office. He said that there must be something wrong with me that I was struggling at PE. I was stung to the core. He had no idea what was going on with me at my company, yet he was making unfounded judgments.

This behavior was not what any religious order should inculcate. Empathy is one of the first things that any religion teaches. I was cheesed off. Here I was really struggling in Atlanta and here was this guy adding salt to my wounds. And then the guy told me to quit bitching about Atlanta. I told him that I never did so, it was only the president who kept bringing up how hard Atlanta must be for me. Mercifully, she accepted how she behaved. Then an old Indian lady asked me if I spoke Hindi. This was once again Indian color prejudice at its best. As I have mentioned earlier, northerners in India consider dark people as southerners. Hindi is spoken in the north. So this woman thought that with my dark complexion, I was a southerner and didn't understand Hindi. The funniest thing was that this woman herself was not from the north. She was from the west of India, from the state of Gujarat. Her native tongue was not Hindi but Gujarati. Her Hindi was at best pidgin. Hindi was my mother tongue. And then she was only a couple shades lighter than me, but full of color prejudice. I didn't know what to do with the folks at this religious service. Complaining to the Toronto preacher would have been akin to committing hara-kiri because she would have naturally taken the side of her old devotees, the very ones who were busy building a million-dollar temple for her.

I was eager to meet a woman in Atlanta, outside of work that is. That wasn't happening at my religious service. I decided to ask my doctor, my primary care provider, for guidance when I went to see him for my annual physical. Before I broached the subject, he told me that he had to give me a rectal exam to check for the possibility of prostate cancer. I was 40 and had never had a rectal exam before so I readily agreed to have it. The doctor asked me to lie on my side and shoved his middle finger through my rectum.

I screamed. The pain was excruciating. He hadn't used any gel. Then to meet people, he told me to go to a certain church in Atlanta. One Sunday I drove there. The church was located in a tony, leafy part of Atlanta. There were many churches there. The church that I entered seemed strange to me. I looked around. There were not many women there. It was crowded with men. I thought that maybe this was a gay church. I didn't know then that churches for gays existed in the world.

Disappointed, I went to the parking lot. There I met a woman from Jamaica. We hit it off. I asked her if this church was gay. She said, yes. Oh! I got it now. My doctor was gay. That's why he gave me the rectal exam without using any gel and without wearing any plastic gloves. He thought I was gay too so he sent me to a homosexual church. But I had told him that I was looking for a woman. Why did he send me to a gay church? Weird Atlanta! The Jamaican woman was a nurse. She said that she would fix me up with a woman.

The woman she introduced me to was a nurse too. She was white. She had been with an Indian guy for a long time. She had a thing for Indian guys. Her mother told her that she was weird for dating Indian men, but that she accepted her for being weird. Nancy, my date, was attractive, but a little too husky for my liking. We would meet at Starbucks every Sunday. She would come from church and implore me to attend it with her. I responded that she should just tell me what she had learned at church that day and I would imbibe the LORD's teaching that way. Instead she rolled up her skirt and showed me almost all of her white thigh. She said that this would be my fruit if I came to church. I rolled my eyes over. I had seen enough of white thighs. I didn't need white thighs to entice me to church. We were done.

When I had fallen for Holli, the girl I met on the plane to Jackson, Sonya was my ex but still confidante at that time. She wanted me to make sure that Holli was not Baptist. Holli hailed from Jackson, Mississippi. Sonya was a southerner herself. She didn't want me to get entangled with a Baptist. She thought that they were ultra-orthodox. But Holli turned out to be Methodist. In any case, things didn't work out between Holli and me.

In Silicon Valley, in the Midwest, in Texas I would see churches of all denominations: Baptist, Methodist, Presbyterian, Episcopalian, Catholic. In Atlanta, I only saw Baptist churches at every corner. Southern Baptist. Korean Baptist. Peachtree Baptist. I wondered where all the other denominations had gone. Sonya had put the fear of the Baptist church in me. I lived in a suburb of Atlanta called Dunwoody. My neck used to hurt those days. I was looking for a place to swim. The Dunwoody Baptist Church had a gym attached to it with a decent swimming pool. I signed up immediately. I started playing basketball there too later. It was loads of fun. All of the staff was very kind to me. One got me a $10 discount off one's monthly membership if one attended the church's service, which I started doing. It was pure heaven being there. I don't know what Sonya was talking about Baptist churches being ultra-conservative and perhaps even racist. I never encountered anything like that there. The church was a mile from my house so I started walking to it instead of taking the car.

I realized by now how unkind and unfeeling my Hindu group had become. It had morphed into a kind of cult. I was accepted for who I was at the church but constantly derided at my Hindu group. The preacher in Toronto realized that I was a good writer in English. She tasked me with translating Sanskrit scriptures into English. Sanskrit is to Hindi what Latin is to English. I didn't understand any of it. I would have to cut and paste letters and words from her document into an online Sanskrit-English dictionary. It was a tedious process. Soon enough I was spending 10 hours a day working on her material. It took me about two weeks to finish the first set she gave me. I thought I had done a mighty fine job but she wasn't happy. She sent me a 100-page Sanskrit book to translate. I thought if she was unhappy with my work, why was she plying more work on me? Appreciation was at a loss to be found in the cult.

I pleaded with the preacher. I said that I was looking for a job and trying to start my own business. That left me with no time for anything else. But my pleas had no effect on her. She wanted her work done. The cult seemed to relegate all matters pertaining to one's bread and butter as temporal issues to be ignored willfully, which God would take care of on His own. But no god ever asks you to be careless and irresponsible when it comes to your daily needs. In fact, a good God like Jesus makes you verily cognizant of your worldly responsibilities.

In addition, there were the constant importunities for money. The preacher from Toronto wanted money for her temple. The preacher from India who was building a Sanskrit university there wanted money. The temple in Austin wanted money for its maintenance. I had lost my job once again. How in high heavens was I going to fulfill all these demands? I wrote to all of the preachers requesting them to ease the burden on me. But none of them responded. They would just take, take, take, and not even bother to respond. A preacher from Austin rang me up. I bawled my heart out to her. She didn't approve of what the other preachers were doing but in the final analysis she had called me only to solicit me for more money. Oof!

I had had enough. I went to one last service in Atlanta, where everyone made me very uncomfortable. I decided to bow out of the Hindu group. I realize now that whosoever they would exclude from their cult, they would bad mouth. They would never say any good things about the excluded. They would hold the wrath of the Devil over your head if you left the cult. That you would go mad. That you would fall sick. That you would go bankrupt. That you would die. Well, I was going bankrupt feeding the cult. How much more bankrupt could I become? I felt so insulted that I asked the president of the Atlanta chapter to refund me my $500 life membership with her, but she refused to do so. I wrote her boss, the Toronto preacher, for the money but she didn't reply either. It wasn't the money for me. It was the principle. $500 was in any case a small amount when compared to the amount of money I had donated to the cult. The principle was that if I am a member, and if you are forcing me to leave for no fault of mine except that I won't participate in the construction of your million-dollar temple, then at least refund my membership dues for excluding me from your group. My entreaties fell on deaf ears.

CHAPTER 10

The First Real Come
to Jesus Moment

I was scalded by my Hindu experience. No one should behave like this with another, let alone people belonging to the same religious congregation. I didn't know what I had done to deserve my fate. I had provided all kinds of service—monetary and physical and mental. I had imbibed the teachings of the guru. Instead of holding me up as a role model, martinets had made a mockery out of me and made me flee. I was now well and truly lost in Atlanta. I had no job. My neck hurt like hell. I signed up with a physical therapist at the Baptist church fitness center. My therapist was Methodist. She didn't care for the Baptists, especially the fact that they didn't drink. She gave me hard-core exercises to do for my neck, which had little to no effect.

I fell grievously ill. I used to sleep all day, eat nothing, and then at night, ravenous, would walk to a nearby gas station where I would buy some cold coffee and a piece of cake. This condition went on for two weeks. I had no insurance so I did not go to see the doctor. Later on it was diagnosed that I had contracted hepatitis. Around the same time a small solar energy company had invited me to Boston for an interview. I asked them for a postponement. They gave me a week's time. I was still weak as I flew to Boston. The flight passed away uneventfully. In that one day in Boston, I would experience the miracle of Jesus. I would learn that what the LORD taketh away with one hand, he giveth with the other. The interview was on the 50th floor of a building called the John Hancock tower in downtown Boston.

Most white people in Atlanta are ruddy from constant exposure to the sun. The folks in Boston, not so. They were pale as pale can be. It was as if the blood had been seeped out from their cheeks, as if they were the ghosts of the people back in Atlanta. I realized then that it must be cold and raining and overcast in Boston often. Not a very enticing prospect. But I still needed a job. I rode the elevator to the 50th floor. The company was tiny. It had a small corner office that resembled a cube. Any moment now it seemed that the cube would fall off from the building. Most of the workers were very young and were working very intensely. A start-up then it was. Oh, my LORD, that could mean 16-hour work days. I had put those in before and knew the toll that they had taken on my personal life.

I was 42 now and really wanted to get married and start a family. But with such long work hours, how would I get the time to meet anyone? I knew no one in Boston. With such gloomy, unenticing thoughts I entered the interview room. I looked out of the large glass windows. Boston was red and gritty. The first interviewer arrived. He was about 60 and had a walrus moustache. I had been to countless interviews where the interviewers had raked me over the coals. Not so this man. He seemed to be a gentleman. He told me to allow him to talk first for 10 minutes and then I could have my turn. I had been taught by a professional career coach that whenever an interviewer wanted to talk, to let them do so. That way they almost always felt that the interview had gone well. Not that I had any choice in the matter here.

Wrapping up his spiel, the kindly man asked me to begin mine. But no words came out of my mouth. I just couldn't say anything. Come on, I goaded myself. You have done this thing a million times before. I felt alternately hot and cold in my woolen suit. Even as I write this, I can recall the horror of that moment. My feet started sweating. I kicked my shoes off. Finally after a couple minutes, I blurted something. But my interviewer realized that there was something wrong with me. I too realized the same but didn't know what it was. I had never been through such a horrid experience. The next interviewer came in. He was all accolades for what I had achieved professionally. But professional accomplishments were the least things that were on my mind just then. I just wanted to flee the building. I thought my condition had something to do with heights. I thought the height at which the room was located had given me the heebie-jeebies. I had always thought that I was a bit scared of heights.

Out on the top of tall buildings like the CN Tower in Toronto or the Sears Tower (now called Willis Tower) in Chicago, I had always felt a tickle up my rectum. I thought that that was a sign of my being afraid of heights, until a therapist disabused me of the notion some years ago. She said that many people got ticklish in their anus when on top of skyscrapers. But at that time in Boston, I didn't know any better. I was facing the large glass windows. Before the third and final interviewer came in, I went to the rest room to wash up. A young man who worked at the company had wheeled in his mountain bike into the rest room. Only in America, I thought. A mountain bike in the rest room of the 50th floor of a building. By now I really wanted to quit interviewing. But if I told them that I didn't want to proceed, they might refuse to reimburse my travel expenses. I returned to the interview room.

But this time I faced the whiteboard, with my back to the windows. I thought if I could block the view out, I would start feeling better. No such luck. The final interviewer was the boss of the company. He went to the whiteboard and droned on for an hour and a half. I didn't utter a pipsqueak. Finally the torture was over. The boss told me that they would let me know the outcome of the interviews. I couldn't have cared less. I rushed out in a jiffy, took the elevator to the ground floor, and hailed a cab to the airport. My mother phoned me from India. I did not say anything to her in great depth except that I had become somewhat tense during the interview. She counseled me to start meditation. My flight was delayed by a couple of hours. I had never had problems flying before. I believed myself to be the calmest passenger around. Then, I didn't even know what turbulence was. If I had had a problem with heights in the building, now I was sure to have issues flying. That's what I thought.

If I had known that flying back to Atlanta would have instilled such a fear of flying in me and changed my world forever, I would have cancelled my plane ticket and taken the train to Atlanta. The company surely would not have reimbursed me for the train and a possible day's hotel stay in Boston or somewhere in between Boston and Atlanta. But I shouldn't have cared. I should have paid for the train and hotel out of my own pocket. But I was running low on funds and did care. So I decided to board the plane no matter what. I didn't realize it then but I was going through the throes of a crippling panic attack. At the time I didn't even know what a panic attack was.

I asked someone at the airport where a quiet place to meditate was. He pointed to a chapel nearby. Boston airport is one of the worst airports in the world. It is truly hideous. Most Third World country airports are better than it. But it has one redeeming feature. It has a beautiful Catholic chapel. I approached it. There was no one inside. I went in. It was similar to the school chapels of my childhood. There was Jesus on the Cross. There were the images of the Virgin Mary, the Madonna. I felt at ease immediately. So I thought that it was the height of the building after all that had caused me such unease. No, that would prove not to be the case, but the chapel was very comforting.

I went right to the front of the chapel and sat down on a pew there. I just kept looking at Jesus. I had a couple of hours to kill. But just looking at Jesus was getting to be boring. But then I saw the Twelve Stations. I approached each one and one by one read what each one had to say. The whole panoply of images made an indelible impression on my mind. Two hours elapsed. It was time to board the plane. I handed in my ticket and rushed to take my seat. A mother and her young daughter were seated next to me. Normally I am very chatty on flights. But the woman was

preoccupied with her daughter. I hailed a flight steward and concocted a story that I was very nervous because I was going for an
interview. Would he check on me from time to time? That was the
last I heard from him. He must have thought that I was crazy and
his job was not that of a therapist. I was sweating once again and
profusely. I kicked my shoes off. But time just wouldn't pass. Taking the plane while going through a panic attack instilled a terrible
fear of flying in me, which persists to this day. I went to the toilet
to wash up, and soon as I flushed the commode, I felt that I too
would get flushed down with the paper. I didn't know what to do.
I prayed to Jesus.

And then it struck me. Those days I was writing a lot for
American newspapers. I pulled out my notebook and pen and
started writing what I had experienced in the chapel. The flight
was around three hours long. I must have written some thirty
pages, single-spaced, by hand. I just wrote and wrote to drive away
the demons in my head. I still retain that notebook with me. It
saved me, otherwise I would have probably made the pilot make
an emergency landing. How embarrassing would that have been.
Jesus had saved me the blushes! The pilot soon announced that the
plane was about to land. I was so relieved. Now the woman seated
next to me wanted to talk. Now I just wanted to flee the plane. It
was a warm, sticky summer evening in Atlanta. I had never been
so glad to be back in my home city. My apartment was on the
ground floor. Everything would resolve itself soon or so I thought.
I had left early in the morning and returned the same evening. I
asked the cabbie how the day had been in Atlanta. He said that it
had rained. Oh Atlanta, how much I loved you then. I could smell
the freshness from the rain. In Atlanta, or anywhere else for that
matter, I wouldn't have to work on the 50th floor of a building. The
flying fear was just an aberration and would probably go away with
time. That's what I thought. How wrong I was!

I reached home and took a shower. I harbored thoughts of
harming myself so took the biggest knife that I owned and placed
it on top of the highest closet in my kitchen. I felt that if the following morning I could just go out and sweat, all my heebie-jeebies

would disappear. From July to September, the weather is stifling in the Deep South. Everything comes to a screeching halt. It is best to stay inside an air-conditioned room. I though had always walked for miles on end during the summer. I couldn't run or jog because that jarred my neck and hurt it. Just walking didn't make you sweat profusely but I am sure that it did a little. My father always believed that sweating released toxins from the body. Right now I felt that I had a lot of toxins to release!

Near my house was a police station. I had the urge to go there and turn myself in. But I didn't. As was my wont, I grabbed a glass of water from a nearby deli, squeezed some lemon juice in it and went off for my six-mile long jaunt. Along the way I met some runners who were sweating copiously and started envying them. But I had no choice but to walk. I returned home feeling not much better. The following day I still had all the anxieties. I didn't want to call 911. My landlady was an uncaring woman. She knew that I was unemployed. If she got to know that I had a medical problem, she might feel that I would not be able to pay the rent and evict me. That's what I was afraid of. I took off for my walk again. But this time I couldn't resist the urge to approach the police station.

I met a kindly old cop there who told me that I needn't have come to the station. I could have just dialed 911. In any case he heard me out and called an ambulance. Along with me they put a man to make sure that I did no harm to myself or to others. At the hospital a young social counselor came and talked to me. I had no idea what a social counselor in a hospital did. She seemed very inquisitive. I told that I had a history of manic depression but my last episode had taken place more than 15 years ago. She stated that I was around 40. She claimed that empirical evidence suggested that men who were in their forties and who were afflicted with manic depression got a huge manic episode then. I told her that I didn't feel manic at all. But she refused to believe me. The doctor came in and without asking me a question concurred with the social counselor. There was no talk of anxiety or a panic attack.

The doctor told me that his hospital didn't have a psych ward and he would transfer me to one the following morning. I was to spend the night at the hospital. I hadn't eaten anything all day and asked for some food. It was 11 pm and the kitchen was closed but they brought me some macaroni and cheese. I had never ever had macaroni and cheese before but it tasted heavenly. It was like Jesus was feeding me. I didn't have insurance so I didn't know which hospital they were going to take me to. They took to me the state-run regional hospital. As soon as I entered the hospital, I almost collapsed. In the atrium were seated all kinds of strange people. There was a young white woman whose pajamas were so torn that you could see her underwear. There was a young muscled black man wearing only his tank top vest. He was making eyes at the young white woman. I prayed to Jesus. Where have You landed me?

I was put in a room with a host of other people. I did the yogic pose of submission and submitted myself to the LORD. The staff played the TV blaringly loud all-night long and the lights were on full-blast as well throughout the night. The social counselor here was a middle-aged man. He asked me what a guy like me was doing in a place like that. I didn't tell him, but I too was wondering the same. He asked me when the last time was when I had taken a vacation. I said that I didn't remember. It had all been a busy blur. Losing a job, looking for a job, starting a business. The doctors at the psych ward kept me in there for a couple of days for observation, gave me some medication and then released me into the wide world.

The panic attack had made afraid of even driving. At intersections, I felt the urge to bump the car in front of me. But the LORD guided me. He told me to put the car in park mode at intersections. That way there was no way I would just accelerate and hit the car in front. I had to perform many such workarounds to get by in my daily life. But the LORD was always there to guide me. The minute I felt anxious, I would start meditating and go into the yogic mode of submission and pray to Jesus. I was terrified of returning to the psych ward. Literally terrified. I would do anything not to go back in there.

I took recourse to writing. I wrote profusely. I wrote many articles for the *Washington Post* on energy, which made waves in DC and in the country. My editor was an excellent young black woman who had many pertinent questions answering which greatly increased the quality of my articles. A very senior executive at a top consulting firm in DC told me that after reading one of my articles, he had decided to hire me straightaway. The job would involve a lot of flying, but I thought that with the LORD's blessings, the fear would peter away. But then the executive told me that were he not to hire me, would I write against his firm? I thought that was baloney. A million people must interview every day in the United States for a job. Which paper or magazine has the inclination to carry the sob-story article of a person who was refused a job? In any case, this job didn't pan out. I was relieved in a way. I wouldn't have to fly.

I returned to California, which was my home in the US. I rented an apartment there. The local utility called me for a job interview. They wanted someone to work on smart energy meters. I had the right background for the job. The job paid well and didn't involve too much risk or work. I thought I could coast through to retirement in this job. A couple of interviewers asked me why a high-flying achiever like me was trying to work for a staid company like theirs. Jesus guided me not to take the bait. The bait being that if I started portraying myself as being too good for them, they would automatically reject me. I just said that I would be honored to work for them. I just felt that the LORD was guiding me through the whole process. But the recruiter came back and said that they had rejected me because I had gaps in my resume. It felt like a crushing defeat.

I decided not to look for a job anymore and instead continue to foster my writing career as well as confront my fear of flying. I took a fear of flying course at San Francisco airport. The course entailed a flight to Seattle and back. The morning that I was driving to take the flight to Seattle, I had a tremendous urge to turn back home. But I prayed to Jesus and the moment passed. The flight to Seattle was quite uneventful except that a fearful flier who was in the class with me and who was seated right in front of me broke his seat because of his anxiety. Now I had the back of his seat in my lap throughout the flight. The crew tried to fix it but couldn't.

At Seattle airport, the fears of being left stranded arose inside me. I was glad to get back on the flight back to San Francisco. I am not sure if the course really helped or it hurt. Many of my classmates seemed to have a much greater fear of flying than me. One white girl in our course turned beetroot red during the flight. A woman in my course seated next to me was so petrified that she begged me to hold her hand throughout the flight. I should have honestly ignored her because I was practicing co-dependency with her. The purpose of the course was to rid myself of my fear, not to help others get rid of theirs. In the process, I only increased my aversion to flying and hurt my treatment. The Seattle flight was in 2013. It is December 2020 now. I haven't take a flight since the Seattle flight. I often try to visualize what would it be like to be inside a plane, but in effect I have been practicing avoidance therapy. So be it. Let Jesus' will be done. If the LORD wants me to fly, He will make me fly. If He wants me to lead a life without flying, He will always find alternate ways for me to lead my life. He wouldn't let the fear of flying come in the way of me leading a productive life. This is what I fervently believe.

CHAPTER 11

The Trip to India

An alternate way to lead my life was certainly coming up. An incredible way, really. It was 2015. My mom lived alone in India. I hadn't seen her for seven years, since when I last visited India in 2008. She was 82, frail and clearly getting on. Someone had to take care of her in her old age. I decided that it was going to be me. The LORD had imbued responsibility in me. But how was I to get to India if I couldn't fly. I lived in California, right on the opposite end of the world as India. Even flights from California would take two days to get to India.

And then it struck me. Like a bolt from Jesus. I could, perhaps, chart a land and sea route to India. A ship sailed from New York City to Southampton, England. Could I find a ship from Europe to India? But first I had to travel all the way from California to NYC. I had taken Amtrak once before, in 1991, from Chicago to NYC. But it had been such a long time ago. In 2013, a Harvard professor was very keen to hire me to do research on clean energy. He was flying me out to Boston for an interview. But at the last minute I got the flying heebie-jeebies and bailed out. Frances, a Chinese American, was my best friend then and still is. He was willing to fly with me to calm me down, but it still didn't work for me. Frances cautioned me, opportunity knocks but once. He was right. Harvard never invited me again for an interview.

But if I had known then that I could take a train from California to Boston, I would have. Amtrak is one of the most antiquated train systems in the western world. The journey from the west coast to the east coast if done in many parts of Europe would take a day and a half at most. But Amtrak takes four days. Still Harvard was worth it. I should have gone on the train on my own tab for the Harvard interview. I didn't even need to reveal to anyone at Harvard that I had a flying issue. That was my own personal problem. I could have just showed up. Now I have been to Harvard two times by train from California in search of a job, but all fruitlessly. The professor who was flying me there for an interview has actually even refused to meet me. Frances was so right, opportunity knocks but once.

I suddenly came across a Dutch ship that plied from Venice in Italy to Singapore. It stopped in India. I could disembark there. But I had to wait three weeks in the UK before I could board the ongoing ship to India. I wrote Shobhana, my first cousin, my mother's sister's daughter, if I could stay with her. I had always stayed with her on my previous, much shorter, visits to England. She was married to an Irishman called Tom.

The previous times I had met Shobhana, I had been a successful executive. She had treated me well then. Now I was an unemployed man with a flying disability. She treated me likewise, serving me weeks-old food from her fridge. I was sure I would fall sick, so I stopped eating at her place. And then one day she came into my room when I was lying on my bed and jumped me. I was dumbstruck. Indians, Hindus or even Christians, do not miscegenate with their first cousins. I told her to get off me. She told me to get out of her house. Now I was on the street in a strange country where I had to spend a couple more weeks. I went down on my knees and prayed to Jesus to help me. As usual, He was unfailing. My mother arranged for me to stay with another cousin of mine, who treated me most pleasantly. Two weeks went by soon enough. Now I had a complicated journey awaiting me to reach Venice involving multiple trains and some buses.

Venice is a beautiful city. I would love to live there. I took a whirlwind four-hour walking tour of the city. Now it was time to board the ship. I had to lug my two big suitcases across a big pedestrian bridge. Italy has a reputation for theft. I left one suitcase at the foot of the bridge and climbed with the other to the top. Then I planned to come back down for the other case. An Australian angel saw my plight and motioned her husband to help me. He did so immediately. I was so grateful. Without their help, perhaps I would not have made it. Once again, Jesus had come to my rescue.

The ship was fantastic. It had the best food that I have ever eaten. The service was top-class. Twenty five days went by swiftly. I disembarked in the south of India and then took a train to Delhi where my mother lived. She looked so weak. She had stopped dying her hair black. Her hair was now a shock of white. I wondered if I would be able to take care of her. I went to her prayer altar. Fortunately, the picture of Jesus was still there. My dad's Bible was in his bookshelf. I felt comforted. But I had to be careful. Even though my mother believed in and prayed to Jesus, she did not believe in Him exclusively. I had to be careful that I not let on to anybody about my conversion to Christ.

In India, many of the untouchables in the Hindu caste system have converted to Christianity. That hasn't lessened the prejudice of caste Hindus against them. The Christian converts still engage in menial tasks like cleaning and cooking. Caste Hindus pejoratively call Christians *Christaan* in Hindi. I didn't want to be labeled *Christaan*, so I had to keep my Christianity hidden. What if I did advertize openly that I had become Christian? Well then, endless questions would have followed. What did I see in Christ? What was so attractive about the Bible? What was missing in the Gita? What was missing in Hinduism? I would have liked to respond, what is there in your monkey god and your elephant god and your serpent god and your fables, but of course I would not have been able to do so.

And then there was a strong financial motive too to remain in the closet so to speak. My father had counseled me to fight tooth and nail for my property, inheritance of which was in the millions.

I already had two strikes against me. I was divorced and still single. I had no natural heirs. My cousins were already asking me who I would bequeath my property to after I died. Heavens, I was only 47. I had some time to go before I died. And I still hoped, very much, to have children. The second strike was my old mental illnesses, as well as my flying disability, which was seen as a mental disorder in India. The third strike against me would have been if I come out publicly in the open as a Christian, or a *Christaan* if you will. Oh, so he has left our glorious faith, Hinduism, my cousins would have said. His inheritance come from Hindu forbears. If he has renounced Hinduism, he doesn't deserve the inheritance. So I had to sweep my Christianity under the carpet in India. I prayed to Jesus many times a day. My mother's altar had images of many Hindu deities. But I surreptitiously ignored all and concentrated only on Jesus.

And I read the Bible, but once again surreptitiously. My mother had a lot of domestic help. Each one was involved in the plot to divest me of my property. What would they have to gain? Money. If anyone saw me reading the Bible regularly, they would out me. I could not even keep the Bible under my pillow because the maid made my bed every day. So I had to be extremely careful when and how I read it and make sure that I returned it to the bookshelf in the exact place where I had found it every time I was done reading it.

My primary aim in coming to India was to take care of my mom. A secondary aim was to find a job and see if I could make a life for myself in India, get married and start a family. My mother was proving to be obstreperous. She didn't care about me getting married and having kids. She just wanted me to look after her full-time. She was a hypochondriac, and concocted any and every imaginable illness inside her. If it was not her teeth, it was her eyes. If not her back, then her lungs. She was determined to find a cancer, a tumor that didn't exist inside her body. Doctor after doctor told her not to worry, there was nothing wrong with her. But she wouldn't listen. She would drag me to each and every one of her doctor's appointments.

I was at my wit's end. I didn't know what to do. I prayed to Jesus. He counseled me to prioritize her ailments. Anything that was not serious, I didn't have to go with her to the doctor's. For example, I could miss her sessions of physiotherapy. This took some of the burden off of me without antagonizing her. Now during the Coronavirus pandemic, throughout the year 2020, she hasn't been able to see a single doctor and she's stayed hale and hearty, mercifully. Jesus also told me to stay as low-key as possible. Not to order my mother's help around. Just smile at everyone. He was concerned that people were out to get me, and if I got into a tangle with someone, my food supply could be stopped or I could even be thrown out on my ear. Oh, what hell had I landed into from the comfortable life I had in the US.

Older Hindus expect younger ones to touch their feet. I detest this custom. I was willing to touch the feet of a saint or a prophet, no matter of what religion, but touching the feet of impure people who had committed many sins in their life just because they were advanced in age was beyond my comprehension. My mother fully expected me to touch her feet every morning. I didn't do so initially for a couple months. That didn't endear me to her. She was clearly unhappy that I wasn't following the age-old custom. I prayed to Jesus again. He told me that there was nothing wrong with touching my mother's feet. Life became much easier for me thereafter.

When I say Jesus said this or Jesus told me that, I mean that I pray to Jesus and ask my questions. The answers comes back unfailingly. Sometimes it can take a few days, but the answers come to me. They do, really they do. You should try this practice too.

I started looking for a job in India, but I had been out of the country twenty years. I had never really worked for anyone in India. When I had worked in India, I had worked for myself. I had never known what working for Corporate India or what they like call in India, India Inc., was like. I knew the CEO of a leading electrical goods manufacturer and sought a meeting with him. He readily obliged. My meeting with him was at 11:30 am. I arrived at his parking lot around 11. I wanted to make sure that I didn't miss the appointment for any reason. But what I saw appalled me.

Indians reach their offices around 10 am in general. Many employees were strolling around the building by the time I reached there. Some were out for a smoke. Some for a pouch of *gutka* (tobacco). Soon it would be time for their lunch. Then for another leisurely stroll in the early afternoon. How did people get anything done with such a cavalier attitude?

I thought that I would be a misfit in a culture with such a work ethic. I had heard of and read horror stories of Indians returning from the States who just could not adjust to the work culture of India. Just suppose I refused to take all those leisurely outings with my peers. I am sure that they would quickly label me as a hard-to-get-along person. I would be made a social outcaste. The CEO knew about the problems in his company and also knew that he could do nothing about them. Instead he concentrated more on playing golf than on managing his business. He told me that I was crazy to have returned from the States and that I should go back there pronto.

I tried to look for jobs in journalism. One paper wanted me to start out as a rookie reporter, until a senior editor there granted me a reprieve my setting up an interview with the editor of the opinion pages. The oped editor offered me a job, but then didn't follow through. Another paper granted me interviews but the interviewers were very unhappy to see me in the first place. I tried my hand at smart energy meters, my area of expertise. Delhi's power utility was installing smart meters throughout the city. They were very interested in me because I was one of the pioneers in the field. They too offered me a job, until the dreaded John Doe letter arrived.

I was at a loss what to do. Once again I prayed to Jesus. What should I do? The answer came that I should concentrate on writing books. I had never written a book before, only articles. I had tried a stab at a couple of books, but the effort had gone nowhere. But now an idea came naturally to me. When I took German classes in India in 1996, I had bought a small book written by an American woman who had married a German and moved to Germany to live with him. In the book, she described many of the peculiarities of German culture versus American culture. For instance, how Germans are always dumbfounded by the American way of eating. Germans place their knife in one hand, their fork in the other, and eat away. Americans place the knife and fork in either hand, then cut whatever they have to eat, then place the knife down on the table, switch the fork to the other hand, which is empty now, and proceed to eat with the fork, with the fork's original hand empty now and placed below the table. Germans find this behavior bizarre. So there were all such funny idiosyncrasies described in the book. I decided to write my own version of Indian peculiarities versus the American, and finished the book, about 300 pages, in a month's time.

Then I started placing it with publishers and literary agents. A publisher in New York wanted to publish my book, but he wanted to own its copyright. A book's copyright normally rests with the author. I guessed that the publisher was a scam artist. I think Jesus helped me again here. I was proven right when a few months later the publisher folded his tent. I wrote two more books in the ensuing months, but had a hard time finding a buyer for them in the US. It was very depressing. By now my brother was going full-tilt after my property. He didn't want me to stay in my mother's house, which I owned partially. He wanted my mother to chuck me on the street. He was my mother's blue-eyed boy, so while she kept making me take care of her and taking her to the doctor's, she was carping in her criticism of me to her friends and relatives.

I was extremely unhappy. I turned to Jesus once again. The answer came that I had to return to the US. But return to what? I had no job in the US, no business there, no house there, nothing there really. What would I do there? Jesus said that I should pursue a PhD in energy. I started contacting, quietly, a number of professors in the US. Some were welcoming, others looked askance at me. One candid professor at Stanford told me that my age, 48 years, would go against me. Still I applied to a couple schools from India. My GRE scores were dated, so I would have to retake the GRE. My mother fell drastically ill around this time and I had to rush her to the military hospital. The hospital would not admit her because she was the wife of a deceased officer and therefore not eligible to receive care at the hospital. I was completely at a loss what to do. I touched the feet of the doctors but they wouldn't relent. I then tried a couple of tricks with the admitting officers such as saying that I knew a very senior Indian army officer and even tried to bribe them but the admitting officers would not budge. And then I, sitting there all alone at the hospital's entrance, with my mother almost dying beside me, prayed to Jesus. He counseled me to tell the officers to do a google search on me. The search revealed to them that I was a prominent journalist with a major Indian paper. They at once admitted my mom. I thanked the LORD for his mercies!

Once mom came home, my brother returned from the States for a visit. He made my life miserable once again. I thought I was leading the life of Job. My brother and my mother's behavior convinced me that I had to leave India. Mercifully there was a ship leaving from Mumbai, India to Savona, Italy in a few weeks. I bought the ticket at once. One November night, precisely 14 months after I returned to India, I hailed a tuk tuk, placed my suitcases in it and disappeared into the darkness of the night to board my train from Delhi to Mumbai. Once I was on the train, my mother made frantic calls on my cell phone, about 20 in all, imploring me to return. But I would have none of it. Jesus had given me fortitude. I had to cross the seven seas to get back to the US. It was a daunting task but I would not come back to my mother's residence where I had been so humiliated, humiliated almost every day for more than a year.

The trip back to the States was relatively uneventful. I had done the route once before so knew what to expect. I thought that out of the eight billion people who inhabit the planet, I must be the only one to have circumnavigated the globe like this, not once, but twice. Such is the grace of the LORD. When you put your faith in Him, He makes you move mountains.

As soon as I reached California, I checked into a hotel. I had to prepare for the GRE, which exam was due in a few weeks. But I started retching miserably as well as suffering from uncontrollable diarrhea. I was admitted to the hospital. The doctors said that my kidneys had weakened drastically. I had got my kidneys tested just before I left for India, and they were near-perfect then. How could they be functioning only at about 30% of their capacity now? Doctors suspected poisoning in India. My brother and mother dismissed any such thing out of hand. I had to begin treatment. At 30–35% kidney functioning I could lead a normal life, but if the kidneys malfunctioned substantially more, I would have to go on dialysis. The salt in the medication for my bipolar disorder hurt my kidneys. My nephrologist (kidney doctor) insisted that I get off the medication, but my psychiatrist said that things were under control. I now have to have a kidney test every six months. I thanked the LORD once again for his mercies. It had taken me two months to return to the US from India. I could have fallen sick anywhere during the journey, including on the two ships that I had had to take. Imagine if I had fallen sick in them. I wouldn't have had access to the right medical care. But Jesus is so kind. In His kindest mercies, He let me fall sick only after I had reached my destination where I had access to good medical care. My kidneys got destroyed in India. But now four years later after living in the US, they are stable, at 30–35%. I thank the LORD for his kindness everyday.

CHAPTER 12

The Second Come
to Jesus Moment

I took the GRE when I got better and did reasonably well enough on it to get admitted to Purdue University at West Lafayette, Indiana's PhD program winning a teaching assistantship as well. I relocated from Silicon Valley to Lafayette. My research advisor was a young Indian professor with a PhD from Princeton. He did not seem to be very communicative. The professor who I had to assist teaching a course seemed like a very kindly middle-aged American. He had worked in industry for many years before coming to academia so could relate to me. I moved into a hotel about a half-hour walk from my department.

At the hotel, a beautiful receptionist checked me in. Her name was Shelbey. It was love at first sight for me. But she was already taken. The hotel's maintenance man was called Charlie. (Charlie was not Shelbey's beau, just her friend.) He was undergoing hormonal therapy to become a woman. But Jesus had taught me to love all creatures of God. Shelbey, Charlie and I got along like a house on fire. I stayed in the hotel for months altogether. Shelbey told me that she really liked me. But she was already taken. That was so unfortunate. I would have done anything to win her over.

At work, things were not going so well either. I had come to do a PhD in energy policy but my advisor wanted to reduce my research to a math problem. I realized that I was in the wrong school. I should have gone to a policy school like Harvard or Yale. Instead I was stuck in an engineering school like Purdue. My advisor decided to cancel my assistantship. I became flabbergasted. I didn't have the $70,000 needed every year to continue my studies. I would have to drop out. This was the second time I was having problems at Purdue. It seemed that the school had a jinx on me. I wrote to the president of Purdue explaining my dire situation and my need for funding. He just gave me a runaround. The semester was ending. I needed a yes or no answer from him before the semester ended. Instead he was trying to wait the semester out. If I didn't nail an assistantship soon for the following semester, I would have to drop out. I became sick of the president's runaround and threatened him with legal action. That was when things heated up and how.

The president set his lawyers as well as his cops on me. But I would pray to Jesus every night. He said that I was in the right and goaded me to continue the fight. When I got admitted to the university, I had written a statement of purpose. In that I had clearly delineated that my area of interest was energy policy and not math. If they had a problem with that, they should have rejected me at the very outset. I sought outside legal counsel, but he was afraid to take on the might of Purdue's lawyers. I realized that there was no way out at Purdue for me. The professor whose teaching I assisted really liked me and my work. He told me that had I been a 24-year old, I would not have been going through this torture. Unfortunately I was 48. Age discrimination was widespread in academia. I just couldn't fathom it. If they didn't want a middle-aged man to come to their university, they could have easily rejected me at the beginning on some ruse or the other. Why admit me and then subject me to this kind of torture?

A professor at Virginia Tech granted me admission for the spring semester into his PhD program. Virginia Tech had a satellite campus in Falls Church, Virginia. Instead of wasting my time prolonging my agony at Purdue, I boarded the train to DC, and then took a bus to my hotel in Falls Church. DC mercifully was less cold than Lafayette. I cannot thank Jesus enough for the courage He had given me to undertake what I was undertaking. Moving from one PhD program in the throes of winter to another PhD program still in very cold weather was not an easy job. My professor in Virginia Tech was Tunisian but he spoke perfect French. He acted and looked French as well. We conversed in French whenever I was alone with him. The technical words in French escaped me at times, but I wanted to please my professor as much as possible. He complimented me on my French. But research was not going that great. The professor's work was completely new to me. I was like the old daddy of the group, and the other, much younger students would not have anything to do with me. I felt completely isolated.

One day the professor called me to the department, but the department was closed that day. Even after two months, the administration had not given me a key to the building. A tremendous windstorm was raging outside. I found the only store with Internet access to do my work. But the store was a restaurant and was jampacked. One could stay there only for a while and only while one was eating. I returned to the department and waited outside for my professor to show up and let me inside. Unbeknownst to me, my professor was already inside. I had no way of contacting him for the cell service was down and I didn't have access to the Internet. I walked back to the restaurant and sent my professor an email from there. He did not reply. Finally, after some five hours, someone came out of the building and I was able to enter the department.

My professor was furious. He said that I did not have the dedication to pursue a PhD. But I was trying my best. I had waited five hours outside in a raging storm for him. Earlier, I had fallen sick with the flu and 104 degrees fever and had to be admitted to hospital. But I recovered in two days flat and returned to the department to work even when I was feeling weak. The professor would have none of my pleas. He fired me on the spot.

It was all to the good really. He was a Muslim. He said that there was proof that Mohammed existed but no proof that Jesus did. Hearing this was pure heresy for me. I felt that Jesus had dealt His hand in ejecting me from this professor's world. I could feel Jesus' presence every day. I felt immensely grateful to Him and left Virginia Tech.

I returned by train to Silicon Valley. Frances, my Chinese-American friend, was waiting for me. He had a new cell phone for me, which he was gifting me, and whose service he was paying for and is still paying for after two and a half years. I asked Frances to help me find a job. His old brother, Phil, ran a railroad surveying company. And then Frances's pastor needed help on his web site. I spoke to the pastor. He wanted to exploit me and make me work for free. That was simply unacceptable, and actually unsustainable for me. I needed real work with real money.

Phil had what I wanted. Frances spoke to him. Phil offered me a six-figure job, way more than my expectations had been. Frances told me that he had told Phil to pad his initial offer to me by $20,000. Good on you, Frances! I wanted to move to San Francisco. A friend who lived there told me to move to the chic Mission district. Phil called me to his office and offered me a corporate apartment that he maintained in the city. I asked him if it was in the Mission. He said yes.

But he was deceptive, Phil was. As he would prove to be time and time again during the six months that I worked for him. The apartment was on Mission Street in one of the worst parts of town. It was nowhere near the Mission district. And then it was located on the 15th floor, where I did not feel exactly comfortable. But I got used to the height. What I could never get used to was the homelessness on the street, the feces and the urine on the sidewalk, the needling of drugs right in the open, and the brawls that would break out between homeless people stealing at a nearby store and the security staff there. I just hated the place so much that I didn't step out of my building all weekend. I slept in all of Saturday. I just couldn't wait for Monday to come so I could leave for work. I thought that I might meet some interesting women in San Francisco, but the place to meet women there seemed to be at bars. Since I didn't drink, I never went to any of the bars and never met any women in the city.

I used to take the train from the city to my office in northern Silicon Valley. What with walking and the train ride, it would take me two hours to get to the office. I was supposed to clock in eight hours at work. I made sure I put in nine. I left home at 9 am, I reached the office at 11, was there until at least 8 pm, and reached home after 10. There really was nothing to do other than work and the commute. But Phil wanted me to show up at 9 am. That was fine, which would aid me in reaching home at a more earthly hour, but if I reached home at 7 pm, what was I going to do all locked up in my building? I couldn't even go for a walk outside. My building's receptionist lived in the east side of the bay in Oakland. Oakland has a reputation for crime. She said that at least in Oakland, one got to breathe fresh air. In San Francisco, she said that the marijuana and the feces and the urine all mixed up to create this sweet, sickly stench. How right she was!

I would barely spend any time in my apartment except on weekends. Phil said that he had got a call from the leasing office that I was keeping my apartment in horrid shape. But how could that be? I didn't even cook. I was out all week. The weekends I would spend mostly in bed. I didn't invite anybody over or throw any raucous parties. But this was Phil being just Phil. I felt that he was intruding into my privacy. But as I was to learn, the Chinese, even in America live by their own rules. The company was about 15 people. They were all Chinese except me. Chinese from Vietnam, from Taiwan, from Hong Kong, from the Chinese mainland. I had a close friend, Yong Tian, at the University of Illinois, with whom I had spent an entire summer hanging out while we both did internships in Silicon Valley in 1997. He was from mainland China. I never ever detected even the least amount of racism in him. I didn't associate the Chinese with racism at all. But Yong was a lone-ranger. I didn't realize that the Chinese operated differently as a pack. As is customary for a newcomer, I wanted to go out with my colleagues for lunch, but they told me that they didn't want to eat with me. Every week or so there was a group lunch I could go to, but then I was made to clean up after everyone else. Ah, I forget. There was a Spanish guy in the office too, but he kept completely to himself. He didn't socialize with anybody. There was a Wendy's near my office and I took to eating there every day. The manager of the store was Chinese and he treated me well, but he too was a lone-ranger. Who knows how he would have behaved in a pack of Chinese?

Frances would visit my office once a week to take me out to lunch to alleviate the stress on me. He admitted, the Chinese were super racist. Frances and Phil's only sister had married a black man, and Frances told me that Cain had been raised by his parents. Frances had another brother other than Phil. All the three brothers had married Chinese. Frances said that out of all of his siblings and he, only his sister was happy in her marriage. The brothers were all miserable. Frances said that the Chinese do this wherever they go in the world, the US, Africa, Europe or anywhere else. Do what? They form insular societies in which they don't let anyone else in. And then I had the additional handicap of my dark skin. Skin was my sin really with the Chinese. At least in white society, many women found me attractive. It seemed that all of the Chinese, the women included, disdained me.

One day, after a few months at the company, there was a company dim sum. By now I wanted to live like the Spaniard and not partake of any company activities. But Phil liked the Spaniard and let him do as he pleased. I still had to show to Phil that I was trying my utmost to integrate into his company. I had had dim sum decades ago. Then I was much more adventurous in my food habits. Now my taste buds had turned much more conservative. No more chicken feet for me now. But all these strange dishes kept appearing. Ah, finally there was a vegetable. I picked it up by its stalk with my fingers because the stalk was too thick to clasp with chopsticks. I was scared that if using the chopsticks, I dropped the food, I would end up looking like an idiot.

Someone barked. It was an old Chinese woman, the self-appointed matriarch of the firm. She forbade me to use my bare hands to pick up food. I apologized and just sank in my seat. My dim sum was over. But my Chinese colleagues seated next to me were all picking up buns and other food with their bare hands. The matriarch didn't say anything to them. I guess I was being reserved for special treatment. I thought that even Jesus had given up on me. One day I went to the Wendy's. There was a card lying on the floor. I picked it up and was about to throw it in the trash when I realized that Jesus, sweet Jesus was on the other side of the card. He had not deserted me. I kept the card face up on my office desk. It gave me great solace and strength to go through all the trials and tribulations at the company.

The pay was good and I wanted to work in this as yet new rail industry for me and master it until retirement. My old industry, clean energy, was still in the dumps. There was no hope of going back to it. But Phil had decreed otherwise it seemed. He decided to amp up the pressure on me to leave. He had his cronies shouted and screamed at me constantly. I could not imagine that all this was happening in America. Phil seemed to have constructed his own little Chinese sweatshop in America ignoring all American labor laws. But what if I complained to the authorities? It would be the word of fifteen at the company against mine. The best thing about a Chinese company is never having to work in it. One day, Phil called me to his office and terminated me. I felt so relieved. It was about 11am.

I had moved from San Francisco by then and returned back to Silicon Valley. I was in my hotel by noon. I went straight to the hotel computer and wrote out a book proposal with three sample chapters that very day. I didn't want to moon. And moon over what? Over a horror Chinese story? I didn't realize then that Jesus' hands move in mysterious ways. He didn't want me to hide behind books for four-five years and get a PhD. He didn't want me to be anywhere near a racist Chinese sweatshop. My calling was writing. By now I have published close to four books with prestigious publishers worldwide and placed nearly five hundred articles in global newspapers. Jesus wanted me to launch my writing career and not look hither and thither fruitlessly for digressions. When I did, He forced me back into line. I know that Jesus has been watching over me all along and clearing the pathways for me when needed and putting obstacles in front of me when I strayed from His chosen path. The path that He has chosen for me, writing, I am committed to following even at the pain of hunger or even death. I cannot sing (or write) His glories enough.

By the way, the picture of Jesus I found at Wendy's is always with me. I found another picture of His since and have placed it on on my table and pray to it many times a day. Hail to my Savior, Jesus, who has saved time and time again from sin and immorality and made me the person that I am today. I wish your experience with Jesus would be similar in many ways to my experience with Him. All one has to do is generate awareness in oneself that He is there for one and that He is always blessing people who have faith in Him, and the rest is all magically taken care of by itself. All one's troubles will melt away, without one even realizing it. Now they may not melt away the way one would like them to melt away; but melt away they will. Such is the power of submission to Him, our one and only LORD and Savior, Jesus Christ!

The Pastor on TV

The other day I woke up and switched the TV on to a Christian channel. I saw a pastor, all slicked-up and suited-booted, delivering a sermon. I had never seen the pastor before. Only later did I realize that he was a nationally-recognized figure. He stated that Jesus would restore your past harvests that locusts had eaten. I had by now been without a paycheck, save for a small period, for more than 10 years. The pastor's words sounded very appealing, very enticing to me. I was keen on hearing him out.

The pastor went on to say that even if you had lost your first love, your second love was round the corner. I had been in the marriage market for over 10 years, looking for a good Christian girl with whom I could raise a family. Most Indian women were not Christian and most American women I felt did not want to have anything to do with me because of my ethnicity. I was in a real logjam. I kept myself really fit, but at 52, I was getting on. Would Jesus ever let me settle down? It seemed that the pastor was speaking directly to me. But I knew that whatever the LORD decided was the right thing for me. If the LORD felt that I should get married and have children, then that was great. But if He decreed that I should stay single, that was perfectly fine as well. In either case, I would continue spreading His word and His gospel.

I pray to Jesus about five or six times a day. As soon I get up in the morning, I am before His picture in submission. I say grace before all my meals. I pray to Him as soon as I am ready to start my day. I want my writings to be blessed by Him. I want Him to hold my hand and guide it in the right direction. It's amazing that I never get stuck in my writing. People say that I am a prolific writer. I might get stuck on a word or two, but that's about it. I am confident that until I keep having Jesus hold my hand, I will never suffer from writer's block or anything of those kind of things that writers so dread. And then I pray to Jesus before I pull in for the night. I always say to Him, Thy Will be Done. I never ask Him for anything. I suffer from acute pain in my neck, but still I never ask Him to resolve it. He will resolve it whenever the time is right. He has not let me go hungry for even a day despite all the trials and tribulations that I have faced in my life.

He has not let me spend a night without decent shelter either. I may live until 90, but at 52, I have lived well over half my life. If He has not failed me even once all these 52 years, why should I even think that He will fail me over the next 40? But I do know that Jesus is the Healer Supreme, and so I want only one thing from Him. I would like Him to cure me of me of my fear of flying. Frankly, these two-month journeys to India are getting to be plain ridiculous.

The world is reeling in spiritual confusion. Millions of people of faiths other than Christianity have entered the US and continue to enter it. They tend to cling to their faiths. America is liberal enough that it allows them to practice their respective faiths, without fear and with fervor. It also allows them to evangelize their faiths in America, again without fear and with fervor. But America was built on the sinews of Christianity, on Jesus' message of love, freedom, and compassion. America today is the greatest country on earth only because of Jesus and His followers who built it in His image and according to His message.

Jesus is the only prophet who has descended on earth in the entire history of mankind who has preached purely peace and compassion. His life was one of endless, intolerable suffering. Nowhere in His life did He indulge in any warfare or violence of any kind. He gave up His life, in the most brutal, tortuous way, to atone for our sins. People of other faiths do not even realize what they are missing when they refuse to accept Jesus as their One and Only LORD and Savior. People of other faiths, as well as Christians, will imbibe the bliss of love, forgiveness, peace, harmony, healing, and compassion if they accept Jesus truly as their own.

My book, *How I Came to Christ*, is first of all a humble offering to the LORD. It is, I hope, a small step in the ongoing process of my submission to Him. Along with me, I hope that the book allows people of other faiths as well, not just in America but around the world, to see the true light in life, which is the Light of Christ. I would like to stress that I want to reach out not just to people of faiths other than Christianity. The book is also meant for Christian people who might be losing their faith and want to reconnect with Jesus. If I, born and raised Hindu, could finally see the Light of Christ, so can they.

I want the reader to come to Jesus and not to worship other false gods. I want her or him to believe fervently in Jesus. He will take care of all your needs, and even your wants. You will start leading a blissful and truly spiritually nourishing life once you start coming to Him. You take one step towards Him, He will take twenty towards you. You will start seeing miracles in your life and will realize that these are your very own Come to Jesus moments, just like I have had so many in my life by now. And I know that they are many more to come.

www.ingramcontent.com/pod-product-compliance
Lightning Source LLC
Chambersburg PA
CBHW071138090426
42736CB00012B/2154